2nd EDITION

EASY GUITAR

THE
CHRISTMAS CLASSICS
BOOK

ISBN 978-1-4950-9661-7

HAL•LEONARD®
7777 W. BLUEMOUND RD. P.O. BOX 13819 MILWAUKEE, WI 53213

Visit Hal Leonard Online at
www.halleonard.com

THE CHRISTMAS CLASSICS BOOK

STRUM AND PICK PATTERNS

This chart contains the suggested strum and pick patterns that are referred to by number at the beginning of each song in this book. The symbols ⊓ and ⋁ in the strum patterns refer to down and up strokes, respectively. The letters in the pick patterns indicate which right-hand fingers play which strings.

p = thumb
i = index finger
m = middle finger
a = ring finger

For example; Pick Pattern 2
is played: thumb - index - middle - ring

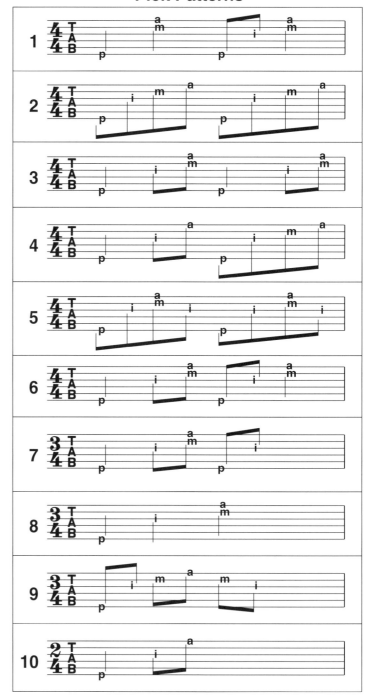

You can use the 3/4 Strum and Pick Patterns in songs written in compound meter (6/8, 9/8, 12/8, etc.). For example, you can accompany a song in 6/8 by playing the 3/4 pattern twice in each measure. The 4/4 Strum and Pick Patterns can be used for songs written in cut time (¢) by doubling the note time values in the patterns. Each pattern would therefore last two measures in cut time.

Blue Christmas

Words and Music by Billy Hayes and Jay Johnson

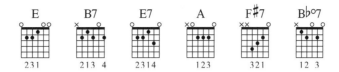

Strum Pattern: 2, 3
Pick Pattern: 3, 4

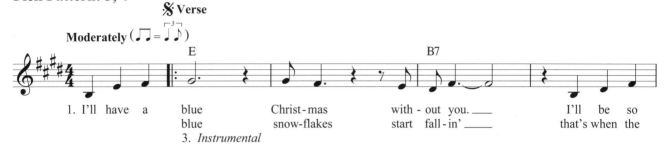

1. I'll have a blue Christ-mas with-out you. ___ I'll be so
   blue snow-flakes start fall-in' ___ that's when the
3. *Instrumental*

blue ___ just think-ing ___ a, a, a-bout you. ___ Dec-o-ra-
blue ___ mem-'ries ___ start ___ cal-lin'. ___ 2., 3. You'll be do-

-tions of red ___ on a green ___ Christ-mas tree ___
-ing al-right ___ with your

won't ___ be the same, dear, if you're not here with me. 2. And when the

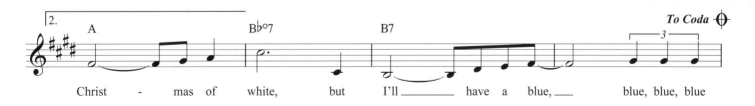

Christ-mas of white, but I'll ___ have a blue, ___ blue, blue, blue

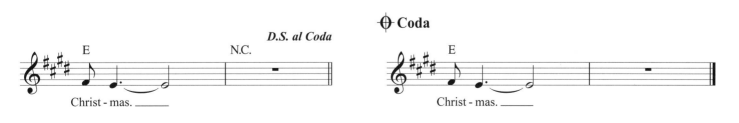

Christ-mas. ___

Christ-mas. ___

All I Want for Christmas Is My Two Front Teeth

Words and Music by Don Gardner

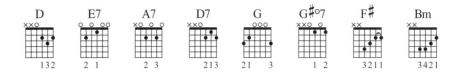

Strum Pattern: 3
Pick Pattern: 3

Chorus
Moderately

All I want for Christ-mas is my two front teeth, my two front teeth, see, my two front teeth.

Gee, if I could on-ly have my two front teeth, then I could wish you, "Mer-ry Christ-mas!" 1. It

Verse

seems so long since I could say, "Sis-ter Su-zy sit-ting on a this-tle."
2. *Spoken: Good ol' San-ta Claus and all his rein-deer; they used to bring me lots of toys and can-dy.* Gee, but

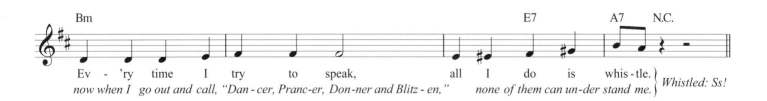

Ev-'ry time I try to speak, all I do is whis-tle. } *Whistled: Ss!*
now when I go out and call, "Dan-cer, Pranc-er, Don-ner and Blitz-en," none of them can un-der stand me.

Outro-Chorus

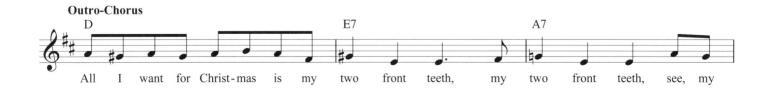

All I want for Christ-mas is my two front teeth, my two front teeth, see, my

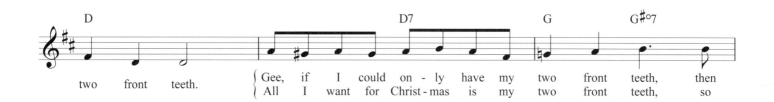

two front teeth.

Gee, if I could on - ly have my two front teeth, then
All I want for Christ - mas is my two front teeth, so

I could) wish you, "Mer - ry Christ - mas!" Christ - mas!" Christ -
I can)

mas. Christ - mas. *Oh, for goodness sakes! Happy New Year!*

As Long as There's Christmas

from BEAUTY AND THE BEAST - THE ENCHANTED CHRISTMAS

Music by Rachel Portman
Lyrics by Don Black

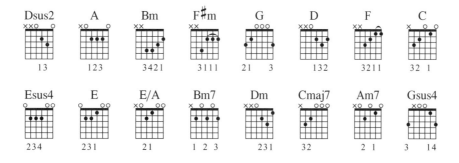

Strum Pattern: 7, 8
Pick Pattern: 7, 8

Intro
Moderately slow

There is more ___ to this time of year ___ than

Freely

sleigh - bells ___ and hol - ly, mis - tle - toe and snow. Those things will come and

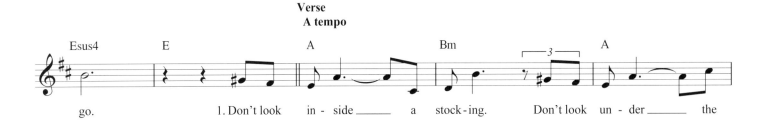

Verse
A tempo

go.   1. Don't look   in - side _____ a   stock - ing.   Don't look   un - der _____ the

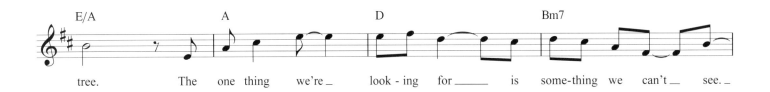

tree.   The   one thing   we're ___   look - ing   for _____   is   some-thing   we   can't ___   see. ___

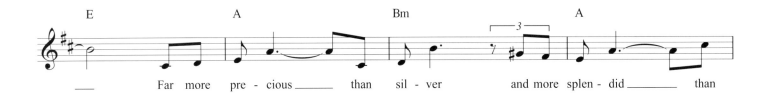

___   Far   more   pre - cious _____   than   sil - ver   and more splen - did _____ than

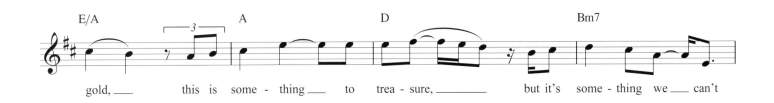

gold, ___   this   is   some - thing ___   to   trea - sure, _____   but it's   some - thing   we ___   can't

𝄋 Chorus

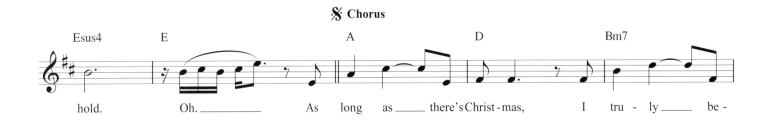

hold.   Oh. _____   As   long   as _____   there's Christ - mas,   I   tru - ly _____   be -

To Coda 1 ⊕
To Coda 2 ⊕

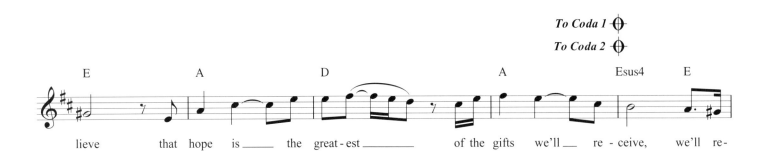

lieve   that   hope   is _____   the   great - est _____   of   the   gifts   we'll ___   re - ceive,   we'll re -

Verse

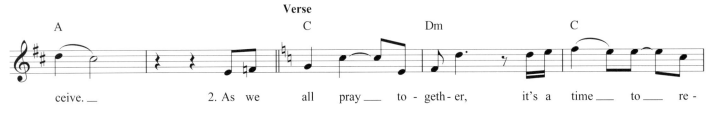

ceive. ___   2. As   we   all   pray ___   to - geth - er,   it's a   time ___   to ___   re -

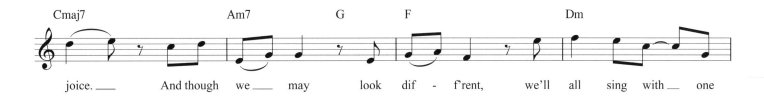

joice. ____ And though we __ may look dif - f'rent, we'll all sing with __ one

D.S. al Coda 1

voice. Whoa. _____ As

✛ Coda 1

ceive. As long as ___ there's Christ-mas, we'll all be just fine. A

star shines __ a - bove us, _____ light-ing your way __ and mine. _____

D.S. al Coda 2 **✛ Coda 2**

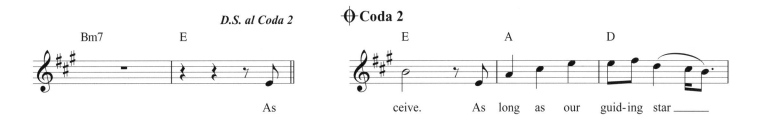

As ceive. As long as our guid-ing star _____

shines ____ a - bove, _____ there'll al - ways be Christ - mas, _____

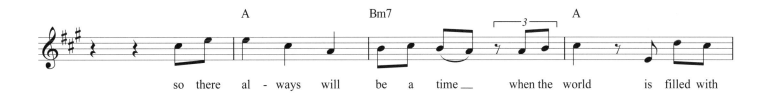

so there al - ways will be a time __ when the world is filled with

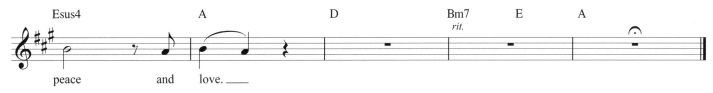

peace and love. ____

Because It's Christmas
(For All the Children)

Music by Barry Manilow
Lyric by Bruce Sussman and Jack Feldman

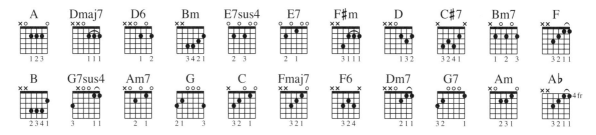

Strum Pattern: 4
Pick Pattern: 3

Verse
Moderately slow

1. To-night the stars _ shine _ for the chil - dren and light the way for dreams to
2. *See additional lyrics*

fly. To-night our love comes wrapped in _____ rib - bons.

The world is right and hopes are high. And from a dark _ and frost - ed

win - dow a child _ ap - pears to search _ the sky be - cause _ it's

Christ-mas, be-cause it's Christ-mas. Christ-mas for now _ and for-ev - er for all _ of the

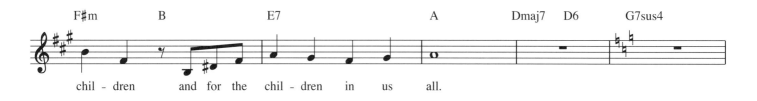

chil - dren and for the chil - dren in us all.

Additional Lyrics

2. Tonight belongs to all the children.
   Tonight their joy rings through the air.
   And so, we send our tender blessings
   To all the children ev'rywhere
   To see the smiles and hear the laughter,
   A time to give, a time to share
   Because it's Christmas for now and forever
   For all of the children in us all.

Caroling, Caroling

Words by Wihla Hutson
Music by Alfred Burt

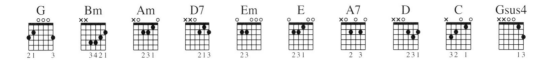

Strum Pattern: 8
Pick Pattern: 8

Verse

Moderately fast

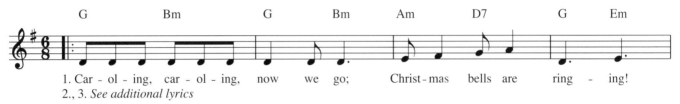

1. Car - ol - ing, car - ol - ing, now we go; Christ - mas bells are ring - ing!
2., 3. *See additional lyrics*

Car - ol - ing, car - ol - ing, through the snow; Christ - mas bells are ring - ing!

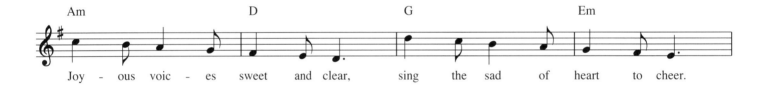

Joy - ous voic - es sweet and clear, sing the sad of heart to cheer.

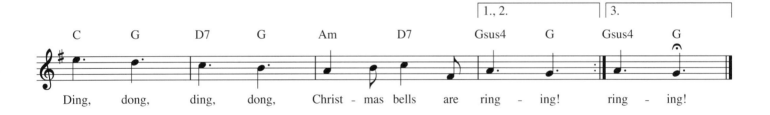

Ding, dong, ding, dong, Christ - mas bells are ring - ing! ring - ing!

Additional Lyrics

2. Caroling, caroling, through the town;
   Christmas bells are ringing!
   Caroling, caroling, up and down;
   Christmas bells are ringing!
   Mark ye well the song we sing,
   Gladsome tidings now we bring.
   Ding, dong, ding, dong,
   Christmas Bells are ringing!

3. Caroling, caroling, near and far;
   Christmas bells are ringing!
   Following, following yonder star;
   Christmas bells are ringing!
   Sing we all this happy morn,
   "Lo, the King of heav'n is born!"
   Ding, dong, ding, dong,
   Christmas bells are ringing!

The Chipmunk Song

Words and Music by Ross Bagdasarian

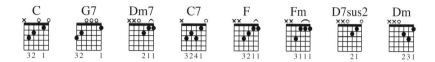

Strum Pattern: 8
Pick Pattern: 8

Happily

Christ - mas, Christ - mas time is near. Time for toys and

time for cheer. We've been good but we can't last.

Hur - ry Christ - mas, hur - ry fast! Want a plane that

loops the loop. Me, I want a hu - la hoop. We can

hard - ly stand the wait. Please Christ - mas, don't be late. _____

C-H-R-I-S-T-M-A-S

Words by Jenny Lou Carson
Music by Eddy Arnold

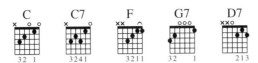

Strum Pattern: 3
Pick Pattern: 3

Christmas Is a-Comin'
(May God Bless You)

Words and Music by Frank Luther

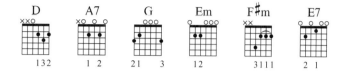

Strum Patern: 3, 4
Pick Pattern: 4, 5

When I'm feel-in' blue, an'

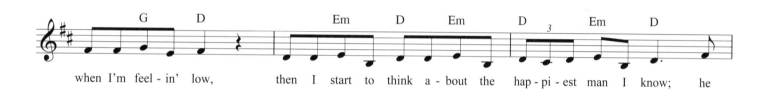

when I'm feel-in' low, then I start to think a-bout the hap-pi-est man I know; he

does-n't mind the snow an' he does-n't mind the rain, but all De-cem-ber you will hear him

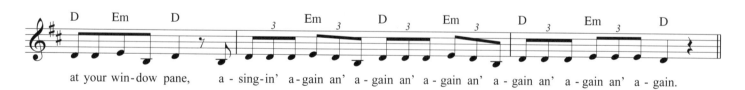

at your win-dow pane, a-sing-in' a-gain an' a-gain an' a-gain an' a-gain an' a-gain an' a-gain.

Chorus

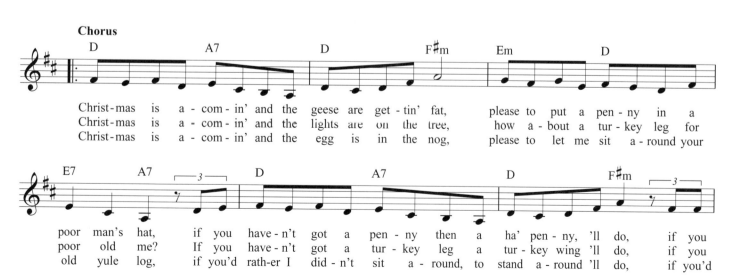

Christ-mas is a-com-in' and the geese are get-tin' fat, please to put a pen-ny in a
Christ-mas is a-com-in' and the lights are on the tree, how a-bout a tur-key leg for
Christ-mas is a-com-in' and the egg is in the nog, please to let me sit a-round your

poor man's hat, if you have-n't got a pen-ny then a ha' pen-ny, 'll do, if you
poor old me? If you have-n't got a tur-key leg a tur-key wing 'll do, if you
old yule log, if you'd rath-er I did-n't sit a-round, to stand a-round 'll do, if you'd

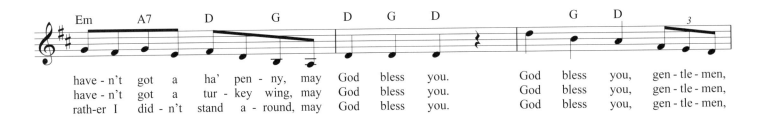

haven't got a ha' pen-ny, may God bless you. God bless you, gen-tle-men,
haven't got a tur-key wing, may God bless you. God bless you, gen-tle-men,
rath-er I did-n't stand a-round, may God bless you. God bless you, gen-tle-men,

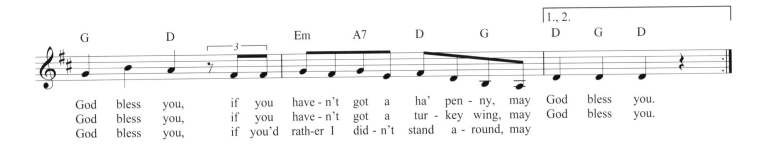

1., 2.

God bless you, if you have-n't got a ha' pen-ny, may God bless you.
God bless you, if you have-n't got a tur-key wing, may God bless you.
God bless you, if you'd rath-er I did-n't stand a-round, may

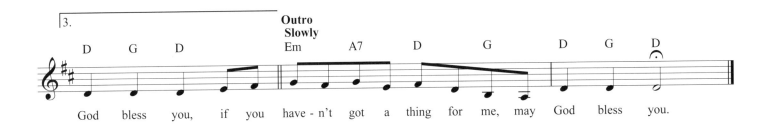

3.

Outro
Slowly

God bless you, if you have-n't got a thing for me, may God bless you.

The Christmas Song
(Chestnuts Roasting on an Open Fire)
Music and Lyric by Mel Torme and Robert Wells

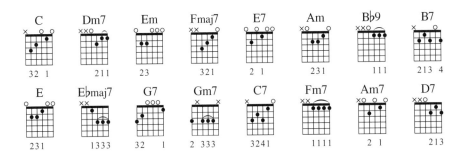

Strum Pattern: 2
Pick Pattern: 3

Verse
Sentimentally

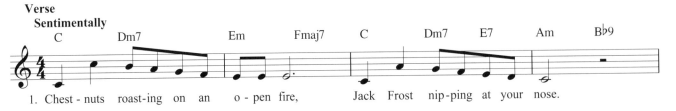

1. Chest-nuts roast-ing on an o-pen fire, Jack Frost nip-ping at your nose.

Yule - tide car - ols be - ing sung by a choir and folks dressed up like Es - ki - mos. Ev - 'ry - bod - y

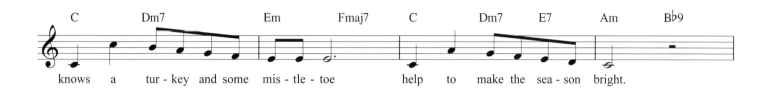

knows a tur - key and some mis - tle - toe help to make the sea - son bright.

Ti - ny tots with their eyes all a - glow will find it hard to sleep to - night. They know that

Bridge

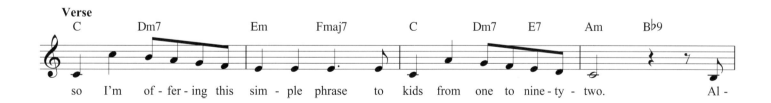

San - ta's on his way. He's load - ed lots of toys and good - ies on his sleigh. And ev - 'ry

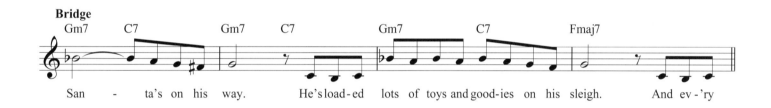

moth - er's child __ is gon - na spy ____ to see if rein - deer __ real - ly know how to fly. 2. And

Verse

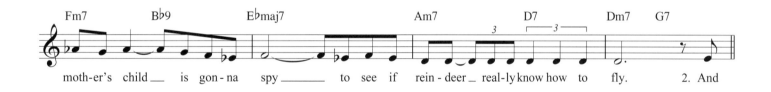

so I'm of - fer - ing this sim - ple phrase to kids from one to nine - ty - two. Al -

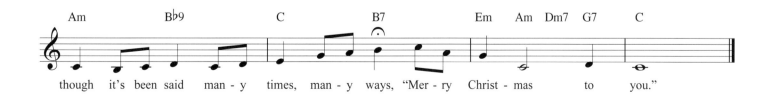

though it's been said man - y times, man - y ways, "Mer - ry Christ - mas to you."

Christmas Time Is Here

from A CHARLIE BROWN CHRISTMAS
Words by Lee Mendelson
Music by Vince Guaraldi

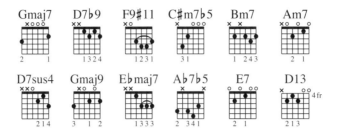

Strum Pattern: 7, 8
Pick Pattern: 7, 8

1. Christ-mas time ___ is here, hap-pi-ness ___ and cheer.
2. *See additional lyrics*

Fun for all ___ that chil-dren call ___ their fa-v'rite time of year. share.

Sleigh-bells in ___ the air, beau-ty ev - 'ry-where. Yule-tide by ___ the fire - side ___ and

joy - ful mem - 'ries there. Christ-mas time ___ is here, we'll be draw - ing

near. Oh, that we ___ could al-ways see ___ such spir - it through the year. year.

Additional lyrics

2. Snowflakes in the air,
   Carols ev'rywhere.
   Olden times and ancient rhymes
   Of love and dreams to share.

The Christmas Waltz

Words by Sammy Cahn
Music by Jule Styne

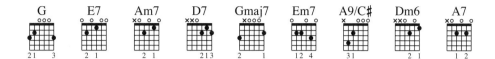

Strum Pattern: 9
Pick Pattern: 7

Verse
Moderately

1. Frost-ed win-dow panes, ___ can-dles gleam-ing in - side, paint-ed can-dy canes ___

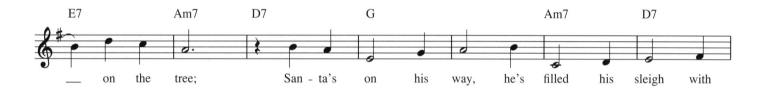

___ on the tree; San-ta's on his way, he's filled his sleigh with

Verse

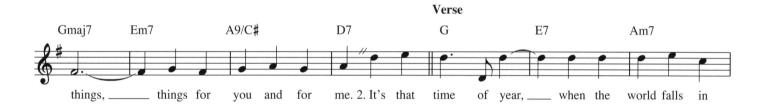

things, ___ things for you and for me. 2. It's that time of year, ___ when the world falls in

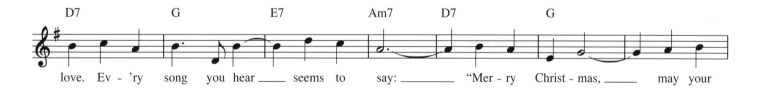

love. Ev - 'ry song you hear ___ seems to say: ___ "Mer - ry Christ - mas, ___ may your

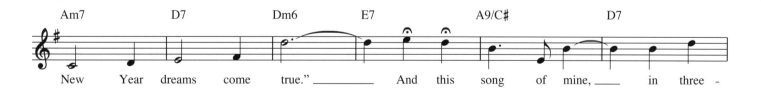

New Year dreams come true." ___ And this song of mine, ___ in three -

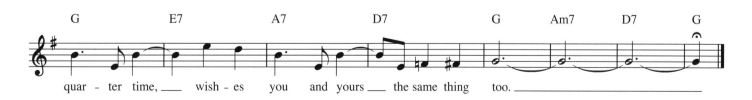

quar - ter time, ___ wish - es you and yours ___ the same thing too. ___

Cold December Nights

Words and Music by Shawn Stockman and Michael McCary

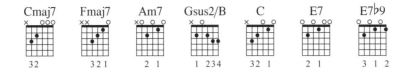

Strum Pattern: 6
Pick Pattern: 4

Moderately slow

So cold, __

so cold. __ Oh. __

1. Cold De - cem - ber nights __
2. The stars __ shine bright

___ like this makes_ me_ real - ly __ scared. You're not real - ly __ there
as the night air, __ and the thought of you not be - ing here makes me shed a __ tear.

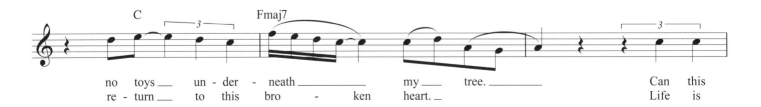

and my tree is real -ly bare. __ An - oth - er lone - ly night, __ no gifts,
And yet mat -ters re - main un - clear 'bout why_ you're gone, __ or if you'll ev - er

no toys __ un - der - neath __ my __ tree. __ Can this
re - turn __ to this bro - ken heart. __ Life is

Chorus

(Why aren't you next to me?) _____ ...cel-e-brat-ing

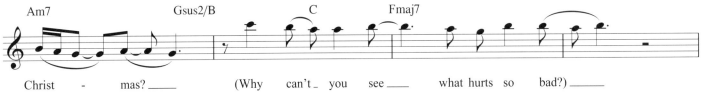

Christ-mas? _____ (Why can't you see what hurts so bad?) _____

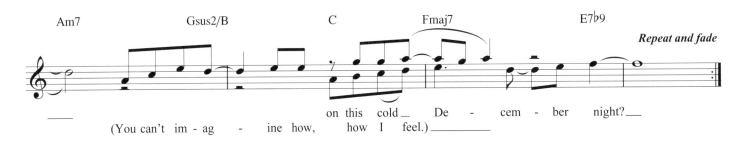

How can you go with-out pay-ing mind to my sor-row? _____

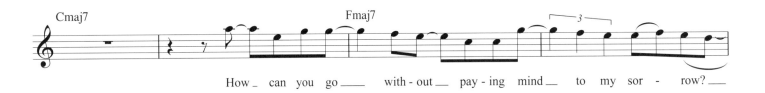

Repeat and fade

_____ (You can't im-ag-ine how, how I feel.) _____ on this cold De-cem-ber night? _____

Do They Know It's Christmas?
(Feed the World)

Words and Music by Bob Geldof and Midge Ure

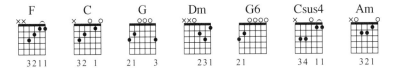

Strum Pattern: 3, 4
Pick Pattern: 3, 4

Verse

Moderate Rock

It's Christ-mas time, there's no need to be a-fraid.

At Christ-mas time, we let in light _____ and we ban-ish shade. _____

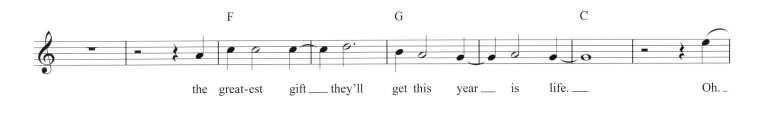

the great-est gift ___ they'll get this year ___ is life. ___ Oh. ___

_____ Where noth-ing ev - er grows, ___ no rain or riv - ers flow, ___

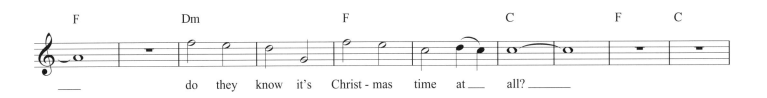

___ do they know it's Christ - mas time at ___ all? _____

Here's to you, raise a glass for ev -'ry - one; here's to them un - der - neath that burn-ing sun.

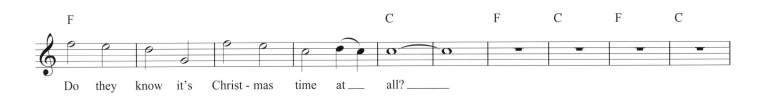

Do they know it's Christ - mas time at ___ all? _____

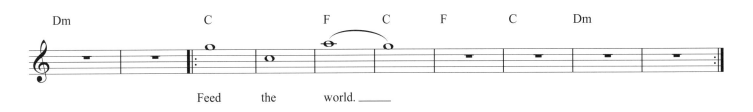

Feed the world. _____

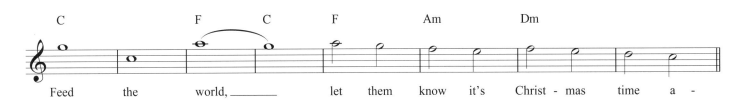

Feed the world, _____ let them know it's Christ - mas time a -

Repeat and fade

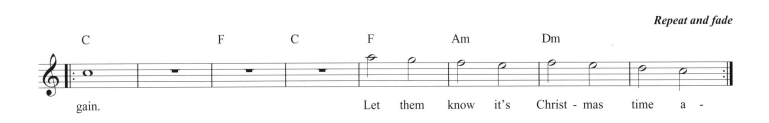

gain. Let them know it's Christ - mas time a -

Do You Hear What I Hear

Words and Music by Noel Regney and Gloria Shayne

Strum Pattern: 4
Pick Pattern: 3

Verse

Moderately

1. Said the night-wind to the lit-tle lamb, do you see what I see? _____
2., 3., 4. *See additional lyrics*

Way up in the sky, lit-tle lamb, do you see what I see? _____ A

star, a star, danc-ing in the night, with a tail as big as a kite, with a

tail as big as a kite. 2., 3. Said the 4. Said the

Coda

light. He will bring us good - ness and

light. _____

Additional Lyrics

2. Said the little lamb to the shepherd boy,
Do you hear what I hear?
Ringing through the sky, shepherd boy,
Do you hear what I hear?
A song, a song, high above the tree,
With a voice as big as the sea,
With a voice as big as the sea.

3. Said the shepherd boy to the mighty king,
Do you know what I know?
In your palace warm, mighty king,
Do you know what I know?
A Child, a Child shivers in the cold,
Let us bring Him silver and gold,
Let us bring Him silver and gold.

4. Said the king to the people ev'rywhere,
Listen to what I say!
Pray for peace, people ev'rywhere,
Listen to what I say?
The Child, the Child, sleeping in the night;
He will bring us goodness and light,
He will bring us goodness and light.

Do You Want to Build a Snowman?

from FROZEN

Music and Lyrics by Kristen Anderson-Lopez and Robert Lopez

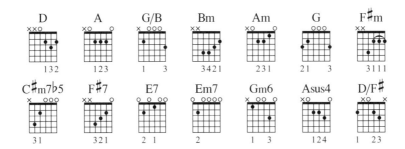

Strum Pattern: 6
Pick Pattern: 6

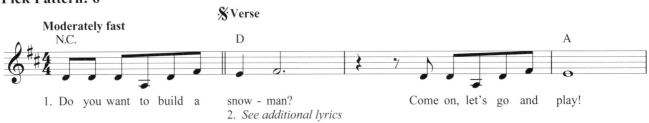

Moderately fast

1. Do you want to build a snow - man?
2. *See additional lyrics*

Come on, let's go and play!

I nev - er see you an - y - more. Come out the door! It's like you've gone a - way.

We used to be best bud - dies, and now we're not. __ I wish you would tell me

why. Do you want to build a snow - man? It does - n't have to be a

snow - man. O - kay, bye. 2. Do you want to build a

Coda

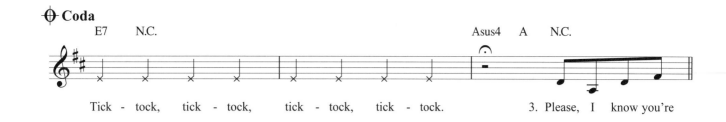

Tick - tock, tick - tock, tick - tock, tick - tock.   3. Please, I know you're

Verse

in there.   Peo - ple are ask - ing where you've been.   They say, "Have cour - age," and I'm

try - ing to; I'm right out here for you, just let me in.   We on - ly have each

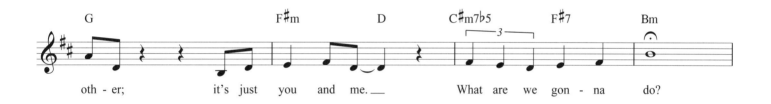

oth - er; it's just you and me. __ What are we gon - na do?

Do you want to build a snow - man?

Additional Lyrics

2. Do you want to build a snowman
   Or ride a bike around the halls?
   I think some company is overdue;
   I've started talking to the pictures on the walls.
   It gets a little lonely, all these empty rooms,
   Just watching the hours tick by.
   Tick-tock, tick-tock, tick-tock, tick-tock.

Emmanuel

Words and Music by Michael W. Smith

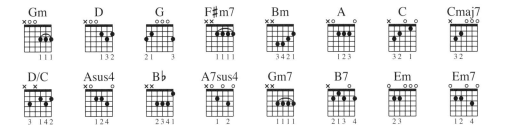

*Strum Pattern: 2
*Pick Pattern: 4

%. **Verse**

Moderately

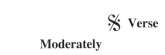

1. Em - (2., 3.) man - u - el Em - man - u - el.

*Use Pattern 10 for 2/4 measures.

Won - der - ful Coun - sel - or, _____ Lord of life, Lord of all. _____ He's _ the

To Coda ⊕

Prince of Peace Might - y God Ho - ly One. _____ Em - man - u - el, _____

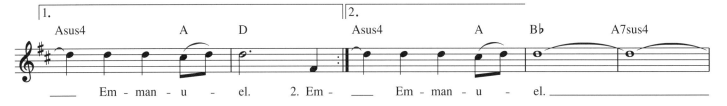

1.
_____ Em - man - u - el. 2. Em - _____ Em - man - u - el. _____

D.S. al Coda   ⊕ **Coda**

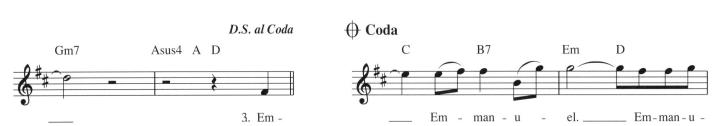

_____ 3. Em -   _____ Em - man - u - el. _____ Em - man - u -

Interlude

el.

Frosty the Snow Man

Words and Music by Steve Nelson and Jack Rollins

Strum Pattern: 3, 2
Pick Pattern: 3, 4

Verse
Moderately fast

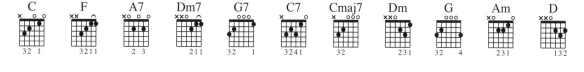

1. Frost - y, the snow man was a jol - ly hap - py soul, with a
3. Frost - y, the snow man knew the sun was hot that day, so he

corn cob pipe and a but - ton nose and two eyes made out of coal.
said, "Let's run and we'll have some fun now be - fore I melt a - way."

Feliz Navidad

Music and Lyrics by José Feliciano

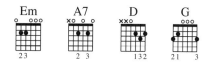

Strum Pattern: 2, 1
Pick Pattern: 4, 2

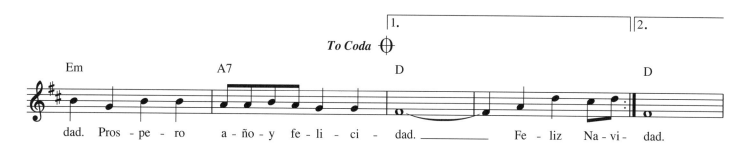

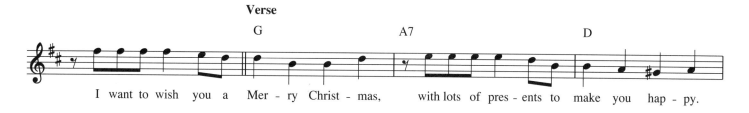

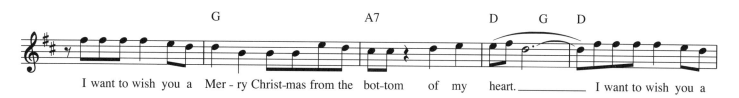

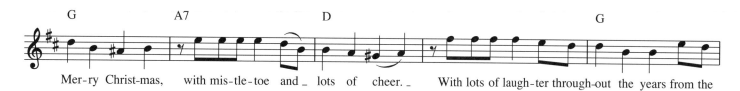

The First Chanukah Night

Words by Enid Futterman
Music by Michael Cohen

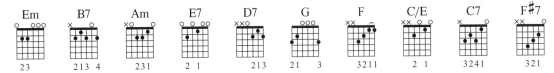

Strum Pattern: 4
Pick Pattern: 1

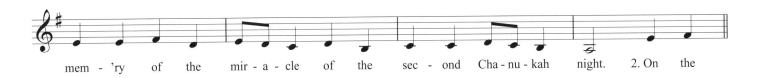

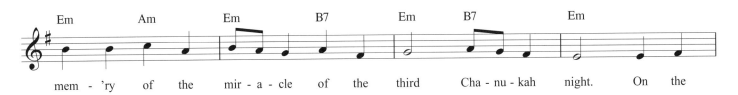

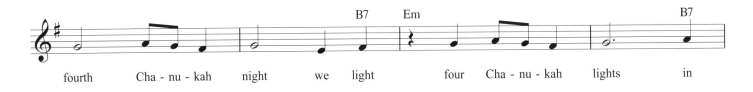

The Gift

Words and Music by Tom Douglas and Jim Brickman

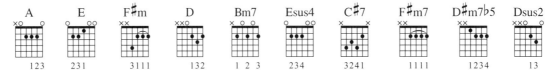

Strum Pattern: 3, 6
Pick Pattern: 4

Verse
Slowly

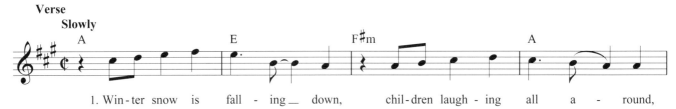

1. Win-ter snow is fall - ing __ down, chil-dren laugh - ing all a - round,

lights are turn-ing on, _____ like a fair - y tale __ come true. __

Sit - ting by the fire __ we made, you're the an - swer when I prayed __

I would find some - one and, ba - by, I __ found you. __

Chorus

All I want __ is to hold __ you for - ev - er. __ All I need __

__ is you more __ ev - 'ry day. __ You saved my heart __

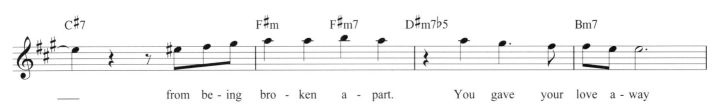

__ from be - ing bro - ken a - part. You gave your love a - way

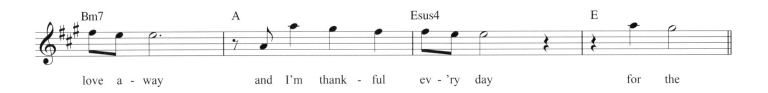

love a-way   and I'm thank - ful ev - 'ry day   for the

Interlude

gift.

All I want

⊕ Coda

You gave your love a-way.   I can't find the words   to say

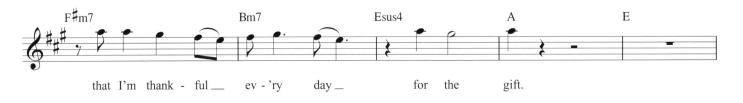

that I'm thank - ful __ ev - 'ry   day __   for the   gift.

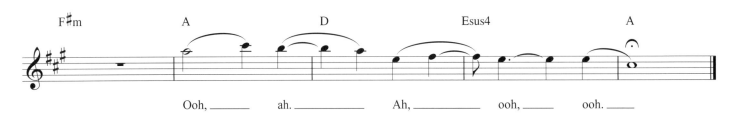

Ooh, _____ ah. _____ Ah, _____ ooh, _____ ooh. _____

Grandma's Killer Fruitcake

Words and Music by Elmo Shropshire and Rita Abrams

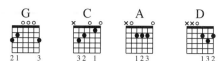

Strum Pattern: 3
Pick Pattern: 5

Intro

Country Polka

1. The

Verse

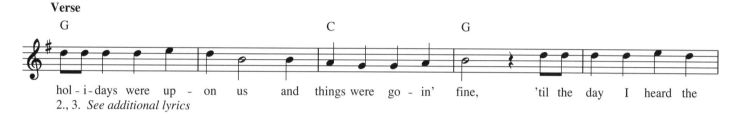

hol - i - days were up - on us and things were go - in' fine, 'til the day I heard the
2., 3. *See additional lyrics*

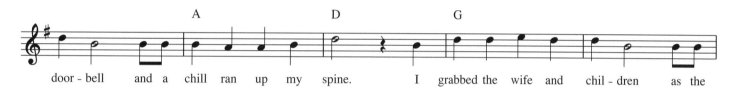

door - bell and a chill ran up my spine. I grabbed the wife and chil - dren as the

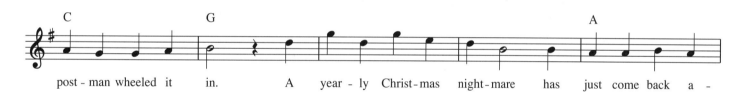

post - man wheeled it in. A year - ly Christ - mas night - mare has just come back a -

Chorus

gain. It was hard - er than the head of Un - cle Buck - y, heav - y as a ser - mon of

Preach - er Luck - y, One's e - nough to give the whole state of Ken - tuck - y a

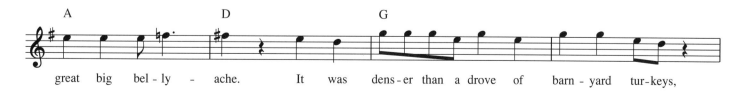

great big bel - ly - ache. It was dens - er than a drove of barn - yard tur - keys,

tough-er than a truck load of all beef jerk-y. Dri - er than a drought in Al - bu - quer - que,

1., 2. **3.**

Grand - ma's kil - ler fruit - cake. cake.

Additional Lyrics

2. Now I've had to swallow some marginal fare at our family feast.
   I even downed Aunt Dolly's possom pie just to keep the family peace.
   I winced at Wilma's gizzard mousse, but said it tasted fine.
   But that lethal weapon that Grandma bakes is where I drew the line.

3. It's early Christmas morning, the phone rings us awake.
   It's Grandma, Pa, she wants to know how'd we like the cake.
   "Well, Grandma, I never. Uh we couldn't. It was, uh, unbelievable, that's for shore.
   What's that you say? Oh, no Grandma, Puh-leez don't send us more!"

Greenwillow Christmas

from GREENWILLOW
By Frank Loesser

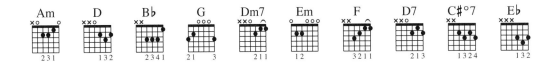

Strum Pattern: 4
Pick Pattern: 3

Verse

Moderately

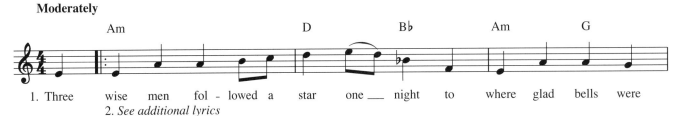

1. Three wise men fol - lowed a star one __ night to where glad bells were
   2. *See additional lyrics*

peal - ing, _____ and soon be - held the __ Ho - ly __ Child and

all the shep - herds kneel - ing. _____ Come see _____ the

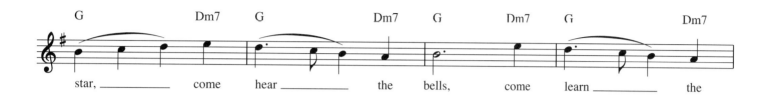

star, _____ come hear _____ the bells, come learn _____ the

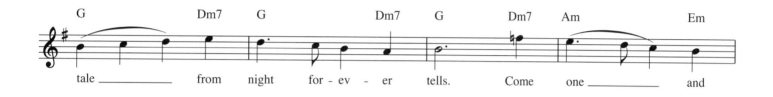

tale _____ from night for - ev - er tells. Come one _____ and

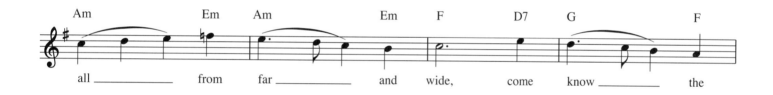

all _____ from far _____ and wide, come know _____ the

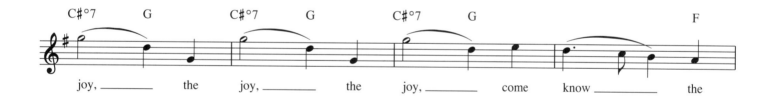

joy, _____ the joy, _____ the joy, _____ come know _____ the

joy _____ of Christ - mas - tide. tide.

Additional Lyrics

2. 'Twas long ago in Bethlehem
Yet ever live the glory,
And hearts all glow and voices rise
A-caroling the story.

Give Love on Christmas Day

Words and Music by Freddie Perren, Alphonso Mizell, Christine Yarian, Berry Gordy and Deke Richards

Glad Tidings
(Shalom Chaverim)

English Lyrics and New Music Arranged by Ronnie Gilbert, Lee Hays, Fred Hellerman and Pete Seeger

Strum Pattern: 4
Pick Pattern: 3

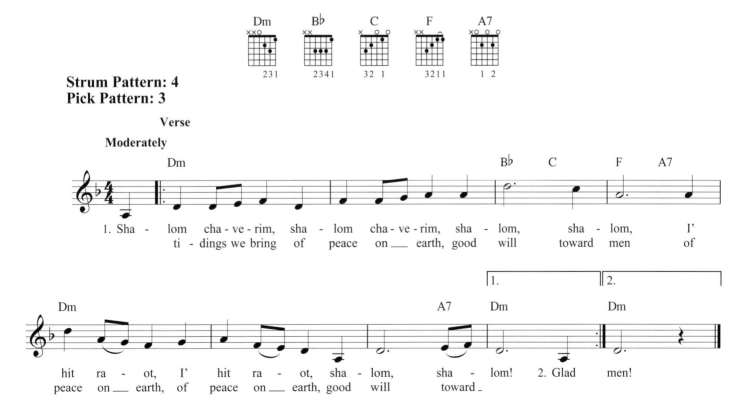

Goin' on a Sleighride

Words and Music by Ralph Blane

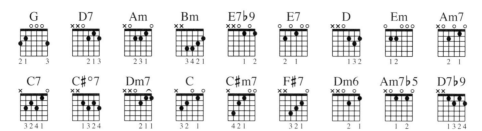

Strum Pattern: 10
Pick Pattern: 10

Verse
Moderately fast

We've got the sleigh-bells, __ the win-ter sea-son sleigh-bells. Hear those sleigh-bells ring-ing merri-ly ev-'ry-where we go. __ We've got the hors-es, __ the smart-est team of hors-es 'cause they know their way back home through all the ice and snow. __ We've got a com-fort, __ a fan-cy quilt-ed com-fort. If we hit a lit-tle storm it's gon-na keep us warm. __ Ev'-ry-bod-y's go-in', __ hearts are o-ver-flow-in'. __ Start you har-mo-niz-in', that's a

Strum Pattern: 3
Pick Pattern: 4

Chorus

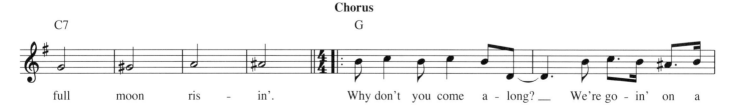

full moon ris - in'. Why don't you come a - long? __ We're go-in' on a

Copyright © 1952 by Ralph Blane
Copyright Renewed, Assigned to Chappell & Co.
International Copyright Secured   All Rights Reserved

Grandma Got Run Over by a Reindeer

Words and Music by Randy Brooks

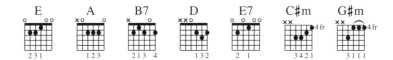

Strum Pattern: 3
Pick Pattern: 3

Chorus
Moderately bright

Grand-ma got run o-ver by a rein-deer walk-ing home from our house Christ-mas

Eve. You can say there's no such thing as San-ta, but

To Coda ⊕   **Verse**

as for me and Grand-pa, we be-lieve.

1. She'd been drink-ing too much
2., 3. *See additional lyrics*

egg-nog and we begged her not to go.

But she for-got her med-i-ca-tion, and she stag-gered out the door in-to the

snow. When we found her Christ-mas morn-ing

at the scene of the at - tack, she had hoof - prints on her

1., 2. | **3.**

D.C. al Coda

fore - head, and in - crim - i - nat - ing Claus marks on her back. elves.

⊕ **Coda**

Outro-Chorus

lieve. Grand - ma got run o - ver by a rein - deer

walk - ing home from our house Christ - mas Eve. You can say there's no such thing as

Santa, but as for me and Grand - pa, we be - lieve. _____

Additional Lyrics

2. Now we're all so proud of Grandpa.
   He's been taking it so well.
   See him in there watching football,
   Drinking beer and playing cards with Cousin Mel.
   It's not Christmas without Grandma.
   All the family's dressed in black,
   And we just can't help but wonder:
   Should we open up her gifts or send them back?

3. Now the goose is on the table,
   And the pudding made of fig.
   And the blue and silver candles,
   That would just have matched the hair in Grandma's wig.
   I've warned all my friends and neighbors.
   Better watch out for yourselves.
   They should never give a license
   To a man who drives a sleigh and plays with elves.

The Greatest Gift of All

Words and Music by John Jarvis

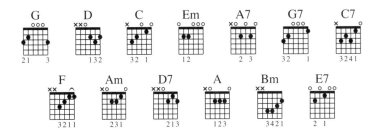

Strum Pattern: 4, 3
Pick Pattern: 5, 3

Through the win-dow I ___ can see ___ snow be-gin to fall.

Know-ing you're in ___ love with me ___ is the great-est gift of ___ all.

Verse

3. Just be-fore I go to sleep _____ I hear a church bell ring.

Mer-ry Christ-mas ev-'ry-one _____ is the song it ___ sings.

So I say a si-lent prayer _____ for crea-tures great and small.

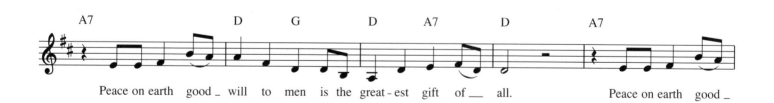

Peace on earth good _ will to men is the great-est gift of ___ all.   Peace on earth good _

will to men is the great-est gift of ___ all. _____

*Use Pattern 10

Grown-Up Christmas List

Words and Music by David Foster and Linda Thompson-Jenner

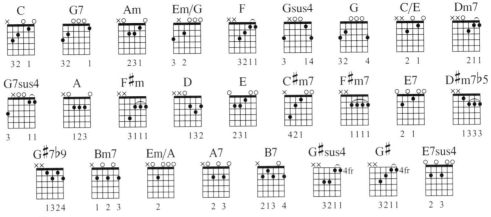

*Strum Pattern: 2
*Pick Pattern: 4

Intro
Slowly, freely

*Use Pattern 10 for 2/4 measures.

Do

**Female vocal:
sung one octave
higher than written

Verse

you re-mem-ber me?   I   sat up-on your knee.   I   wrote to you with child-hood _ fan-ta-

sies.   Well, I'm all ___ grown up now.   Can   you still help some-how?   I'm

not   a child, but my heart still can dream.   So   here's my life-long wish,   my

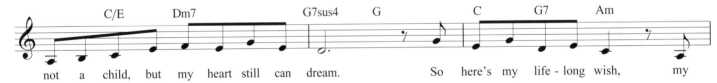

grown-up ___ Christ-mas list.   Not   for my-self, but for a world in need.

Chorus
Moderately slow, in time

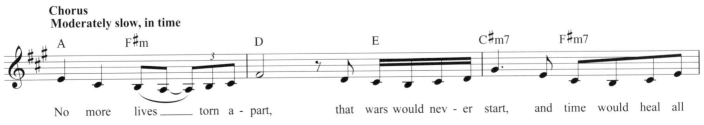

No   more   lives ___ torn a-part,   that wars would nev-er start,   and time would heal all

hearts.   Ev - 'ry man would have a friend, that right would al - ways win,   and love would nev - er

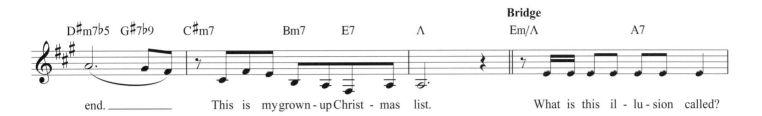

end. _____ This is my grown - up Christ - mas list.   What is this il - lu - sion called?

The in - no - cence of youth.   May - be on - ly in that blind be - lief can we ev - er find the truth. __

Chorus

__ There'd _ be ____ no more lives _ torn a - part,   that wars would nev - er

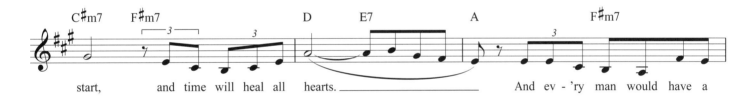

start,   and time will heal all hearts. _____ And ev - 'ry man would have a

friend, and right would al - ways _ win,   and love would nev - er ___ end. _____

__ This is my grown - up Christ - mas list. This is my on - ly life - long wish. _ This is __ my grown - up

Slowly

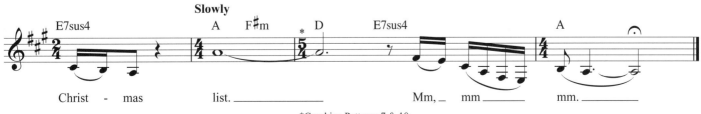

Christ - mas   list. _____ Mm,   mm   mm.

*Combine Patterns 7 & 10

Happy Christmas, Little Friend

Lyrics by Oscar Hammerstein II
Music by Richard Rodgers

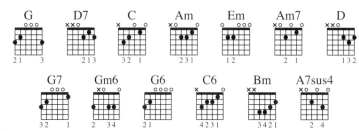

*Strum Pattern: 4
*Pick Pattern: 3

Verse
Moderately

The soft morn-ing light of a pale win-ter sun is trac-ing the trees on the snow, leap

*Use Pattern 8 for ¾ measures.

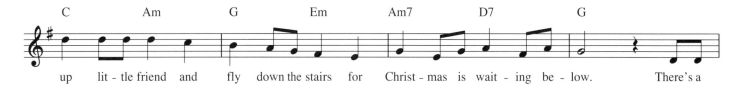

up lit-tle friend and fly down the stairs for Christ-mas is wait-ing be-low. There's a

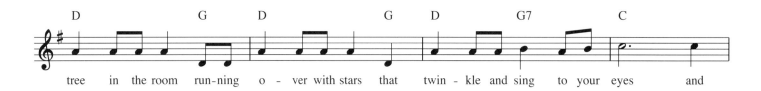

tree in the room run-ning o-ver with stars that twin-kle and sing to your eyes and

un-der the tree there are pres-ents that say un-wrap me and get a sur-

Chorus

prise. _____ Hap-py Christ-mas

lit-tle friend, may your heart be laugh-ing _____ all day. _____

Am ___ G

May your joy be a dream you'll re - mem - ber, ___ as the

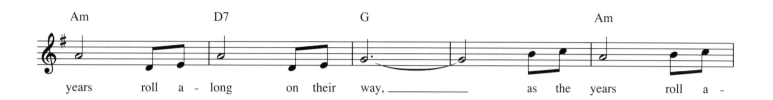

Am ___ D7 ___ G ___ Am

years roll a - long on their way, ___ as the years roll a -

D7 ___ G ___ Am ___ D7

long on their way, ___ you'll be show - ing your own kid ___ a

G ___ Am ___ D7 ___ G

tree. ___ Then at last, my friend, you'll

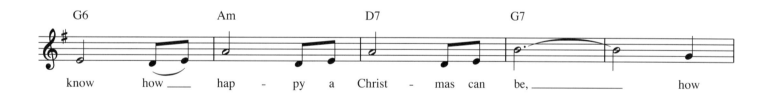

G6 ___ Am ___ D7 ___ G7

know how ___ hap - py a Christ - mas can be, ___ how

C6 ___ Bm ___ A7sus4 ___ D7 ___ G

hap - py a Christ - mas can be. ___

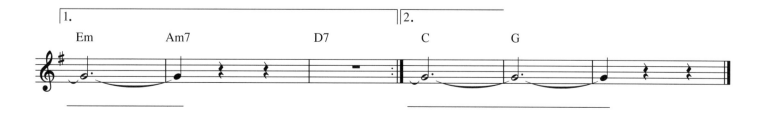

1. ___ 2.

Em ___ Am7 ___ D7 ___ C ___ G

Happy Holiday

from the Motion Picture Irving Berlin's HOLIDAY INN
Words and Music by Irving Berlin

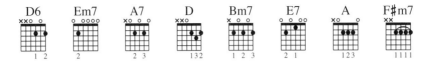

Strum Pattern: 3, 2
Pick Pattern: 3, 4

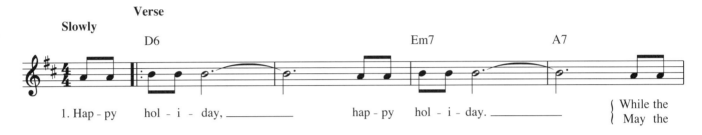

Verse

Slowly

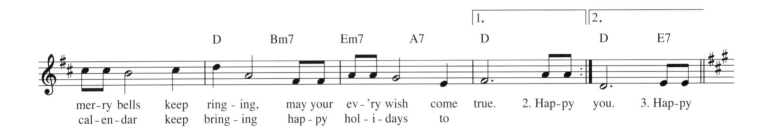

1. Hap - py hol - i - day, _____ hap - py hol - i - day. _____ { While the / May the

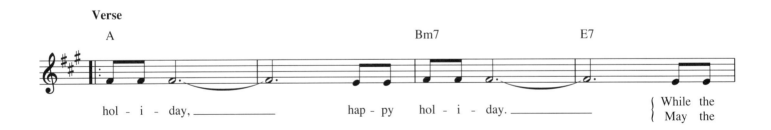

mer - ry bells keep ring - ing, may your ev - 'ry wish come true. 2. Hap - py you. 3. Hap - py
cal - en - dar keep bring - ing hap - py hol - i - days to

Verse

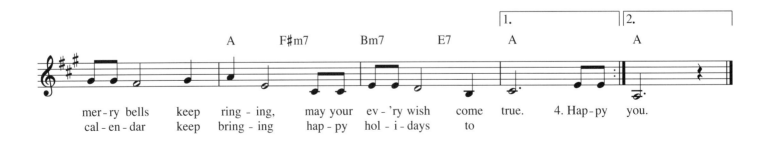

hol - i - day, _____ hap - py hol - i - day. _____ { While the / May the

mer - ry bells keep ring - ing, may your ev - 'ry wish come true. 4. Hap - py you.
cal - en - dar keep bring - ing hap - py hol - i - days to

Have Yourself a Merry Little Christmas

from MEET ME IN ST. LOUIS

Words and Music by Hugh Martin and Ralph Blane

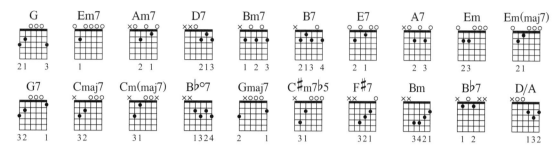

Strum Pattern: 4
Pick Pattern: 4

Verse
Moderately slow

1. Have your-self a mer-ry lit-tle Christ-mas, let your heart be light.

From now on, our trou-bles will be out of sight.

Verse

2. Have your-self a mer-ry lit-tle Christ-mas, make the Yule-tide gay.

From now on, our trou-bles will be miles a - way.

Bridge

Here we are as in old-en days, hap-py gold-en days of yore.

Faith - ful friends who are dear to us gath - er near to us once more.

Outro-Verse

Through the years we all will be to - geth - er, if the Fates al -

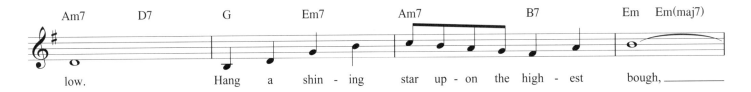

low. Hang a shin - ing star up - on the high - est bough, ___

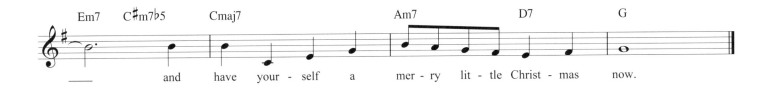

___ and have your - self a mer - ry lit - tle Christ - mas now.

Here Comes Santa Claus
(Right Down Santa Claus Lane)

Words and Music by Gene Autry and Oakley Haldeman

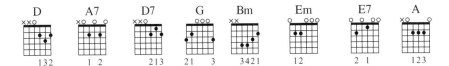

Strum Pattern: 3
Pick Pattern: 3

Intro
Moderately fast

1. Here comes San - ta Claus, here comes San - ta Claus
2. Here comes San - ta Claus, here comes San - ta Claus
3., 4. *See additional lyrics*

right down San - ta Claus lane. Vix - en, Blit - zen,
right down San - ta Claus lane. He's got a bag that's

all of his rein - deer   pull - ing all____ the reins. ____
filled ____ with toys for boys and girls a - gain. ____

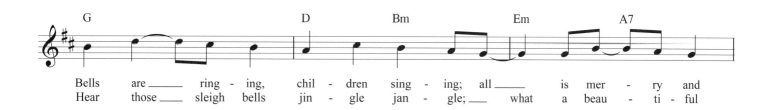

Bells are ____ ring - ing, chil - dren sing - ing; all ____ is mer - ry and
Hear those ____ sleigh bells jin - gle jan - gle; ____ what a beau - ti - ful

bright.   Hang your stock - ings and say your prayers, _ 'cause San -
sight.   Jump in bed and cov - er up your head, 'cause San -

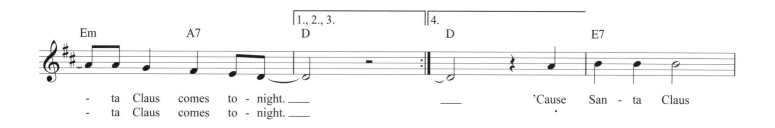

- ta Claus comes to - night. ____   'Cause San - ta Claus
- ta Claus comes to - night. ____

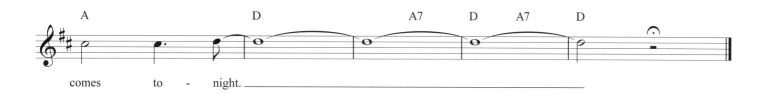

comes to - night. ____

Additional Lyrics

3. Here comes Santa Claus, here comes Santa Claus
   Right down Santa Claus lane.
   He doesn't care if you're rich or poor,
   For he loves you just the same.
   Santa knows that we're God's children;
   That makes ev'rything right.
   Fill your hearts with Christmas cheer
   'Cause Santa Claus comes tonight.

4. Here comes Santa Claus, here comes Santa Claus
   Right down Santa Claus lane.
   He'll come around when the chimes ring out;
   It's Christmas morn again.
   Peace on earth will come to all
   If we just follow the Light.
   Let's give thanks to the Lord above,
   'Cause Santa Claus comes tonight.

Happy Xmas
(War Is Over)

Written by John Lennon and Yoko Ono

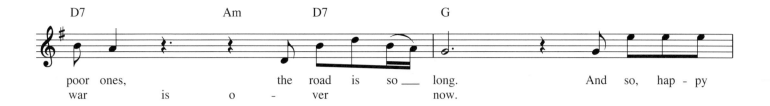

poor ones, the road is so __ long. And so, hap - py
war is o - ver now.

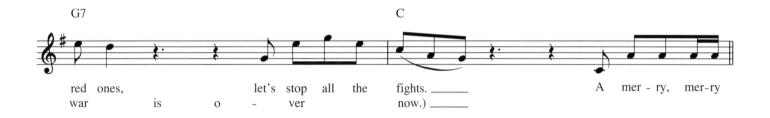

Christ - mas for black and for white, for the yel - low and
War is o - ver if you want it

red ones, let's stop all the fights. _____ A mer - ry, mer - ry
war is o - ver now.) _____

Chorus

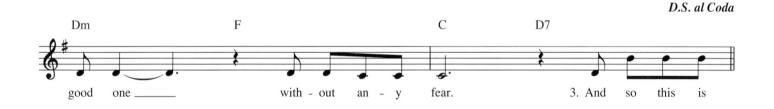

Christ - mas and a hap - py new year, let's hope it's a

D.S. al Coda

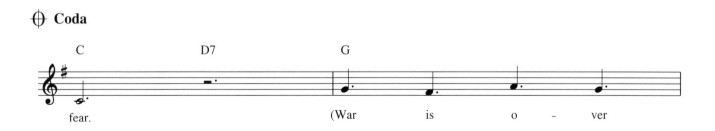

good one _____ with - out an - y fear. 3. And so this is

✠ **Coda**

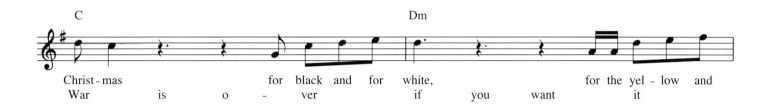

fear. (War is o - ver

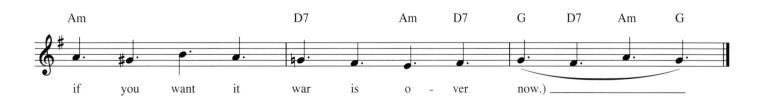

if you want it war is o - ver now.) _____

A Holly Jolly Christmas

Music and Lyrics by Johnny Marks

Strum Pattern: 2, 3
Pick Pattern: 3, 4

Brightly   **Verse**

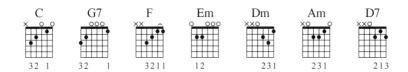

1. Have a (4.) hol - ly jol - ly Christ - mas, it's the best time of the year.

I don't know if there'll be snow but have a cup of cheer. 2., 5. Have a

Verse

hol - ly jol - ly Christ - mas, and when you walk down the street,

say hel - lo to friends you know and ev - 'ry - one you meet.

Bridge

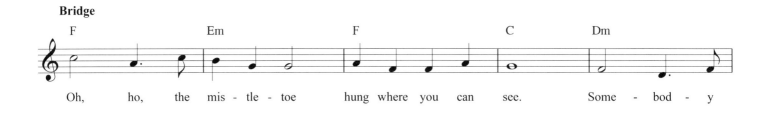

Oh, ho, the mis - tle - toe hung where you can see. Some - bod - y

Verse

waits for you, kiss her once for me. 3., 6. Have a hol - ly jol - ly Christ - mas, and in

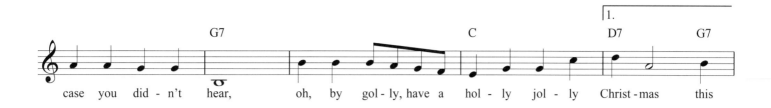

case you did-n't hear, oh, by gol-ly, have a hol-ly jol-ly Christ-mas this

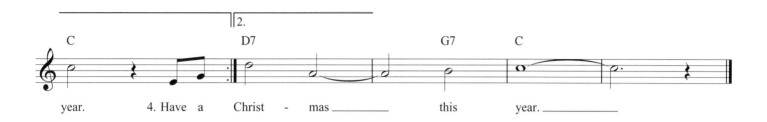

year. 4. Have a Christ - mas _____ this year. _____

Holly Leaves and Christmas Trees

Words and Music by Red West and Glen Spreen

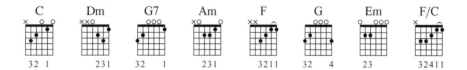

Strum Pattern: 2
Pick Pattern: 4

Verse
Moderately slow

Some-where in, _____ in the dis-tant night _____ I _____ hear

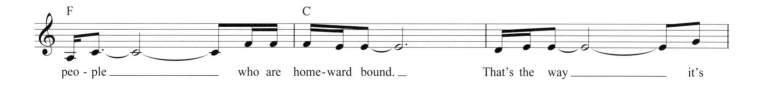

Christ-mas bells. _____ The gen-tle snow _____ keeps fall-ing down _____ on

peo - ple _____ who are home-ward bound. _____ That's the way _____ it's

al-ways been; _____ the cir-cle _____ nev-er real-ly ends. __

Christ-mas seems _____ to come and go, ___ home's a place __ that __

Chorus

I don't know. __ Hol-ly leaves _____ and Christ-mas trees, __

it's that time __ of year. _____ Lights a-glow __ and mis-tle-toe _____ don't

Outro

mean a thing _____ when you're not here. As I walk, _ walk this lone-ly street, _____ the

sound of snow __ be - neath my feet, _____ I think of how, _____ how it

used to be _____ when hol - ly leaves _ and Christ-mas trees __

used to mean _ so much to me. __

(There's No Place Like)
Home for the Holidays

Words and Music by Al Stillman and Robert Allen

Chorus

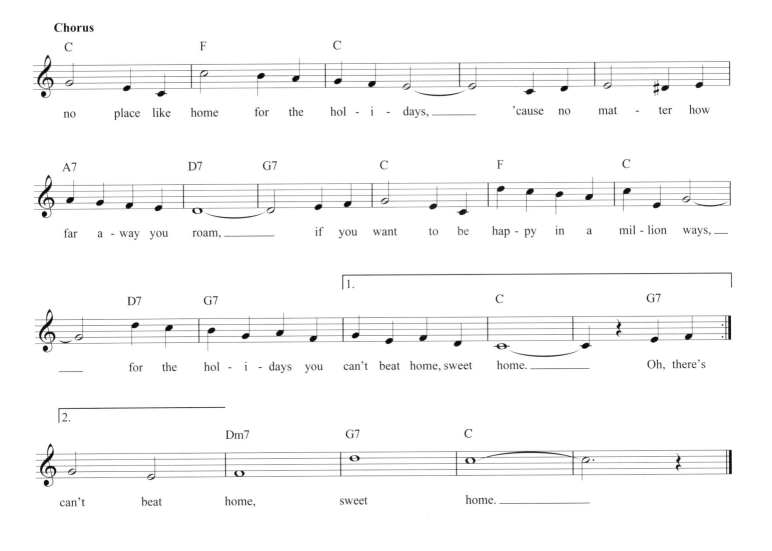

no place like home for the hol - i - days, _____ 'cause no mat - ter how far a - way you roam, _____ if you want to be hap - py in a mil - lion ways, ___ for the hol - i - days you can't beat home, sweet home. _____ Oh, there's

can't beat home, sweet home. _____

How Lovely Is Christmas

Words by Arnold Sundgaard
Music by Alec Wilder

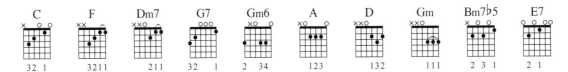

Strum Pattern: 7
Pick Pattern: 7

Verse
Moderately

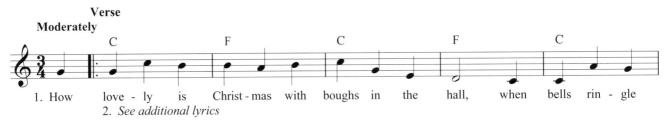

1. How love - ly is Christ - mas with boughs in the hall, when bells rin - gle
2. *See additional lyrics*

jin - gle and friends come to call. How love - ly is Christ - mas with

joy on the wing, while un - der your win - dow the car - ol - ers

sing: "God rest ye; be mer - ry; give peace where you may; re -

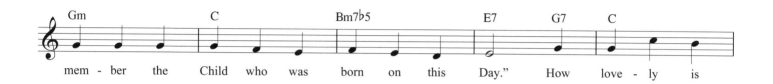

mem - ber the Child who was born on this Day." How love - ly is

Christ - mas with songs in the air, a bright, Mer - ry Christ - mas, dear

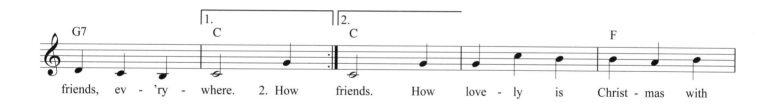

friends, ev - 'ry - where. 2. How friends. How love - ly is Christ - mas with

boughs in the hall, a bright Mer - ry Christ - mas, dear friends, ev - 'ry - where.

Additional Lyrics

2. How lovely is Christmas when children are near,
The sound of their laughter, sweet season of cheer.
How lovely is Christmas with gifts by the tree,
Each gift tells a story, oh, what will it be.
The Yule Log is burning, the stars gleam above;
Remember the gift of the Christ Child is love.
The bells ring for Christmas, our story now ends.
Goodnight, Merry Christmas, dear neighbors and friends.
How lovely is Christmas with boughs in the hall,
A bright Merry Christmas, dear friends, ev'rywhere.

I Heard the Bells on Christmas Day

Words by Henry Wadsworth Longfellow
Adapted by Johnny Marks
Music by Johnny Marks

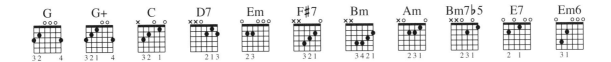

Strum Pattern: 4
Pick Pattern: 5

Verse
Moderately

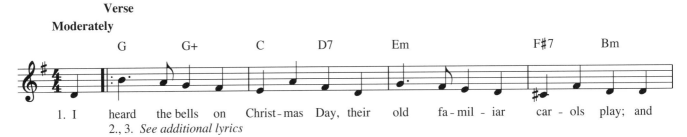

1. I heard the bells on Christ-mas Day, their old fa-mil-iar car-ols play; and
2., 3. *See additional lyrics*

wild and sweet the words re - peat, of peace on earth good will to men. I

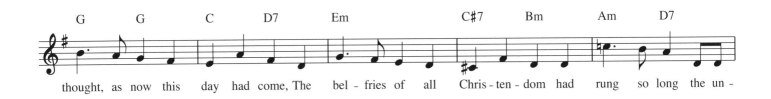

thought, as now this day had come, The bel - fries of all Chris - ten - dom had rung so long the un -

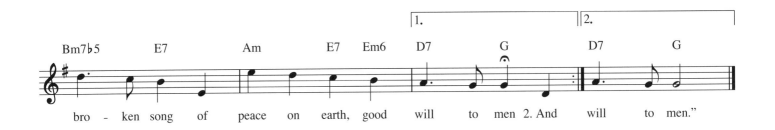

bro - ken song of peace on earth, good will to men 2. And will to men."

Additional Lyrics

2. And in despair I bowed my head;
"There is no peace on earth," I said,
"For hate is strong, and mocks the song
Of peace on earth, good will to men."
Then pealed the bells more loud and deep;
"God is not dead, no noth He sleep.
The wrong shall fail, the right prevail
With peace on earth good will to men."

I Saw Mommy Kissing Santa Claus

Words and Music by Tommie Connor

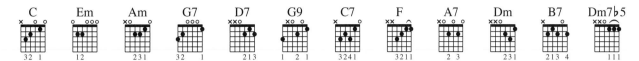

Strum Pattern: 2, 3
Pick Pattern: 3, 4

Verse

Moderately

I saw Mom-my kiss-ing San - ta Claus, un-der-neath the mis-tle-toe last

night. _____ She did-n't see me creep down the stairs to have a peep. She

thought that I was tucked up in my bed-room fast a - sleep. Then I saw

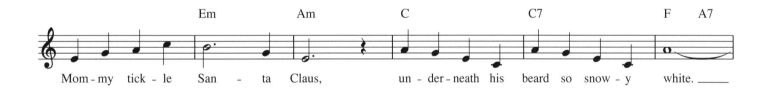

Mom-my tick - le San - ta Claus, un-der-neath his beard so snow-y white. _____

_____ Oh, what a laugh it would have been, if Dad-dy had on - ly seen Mom - my

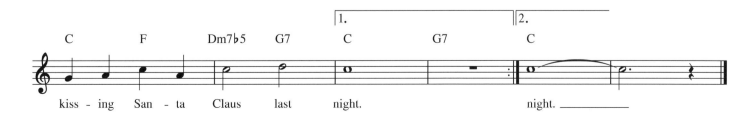

kiss-ing San - ta Claus last night. night. _____

I Still Believe in Santa Claus

Words and Music by Maurice Starr and Al Lancellotti

*Strum Pattern: 4
*Pick Pattern: 3

Verse

Slowly

1. I (2., 3.) still be-lieve _ in San - ta Claus. _ May-be that's just be-cause _ I'm still _

*Use Pattern 10 for 2/4 measures.

_____ a child _ at heart. And I

still be - lieve _ in Old _ Saint Nick. _ Then a - gain, _ may - be that's _ the trick _

To Coda

_____ we need, _ we need to re - trieve _ from a

Bridge

world of make be - lieve. _ Let's make this Christ-mas last _ for -
This time of year is for _ the

ev - er, shine in love a - long the
giv - ing. This time of year is for the

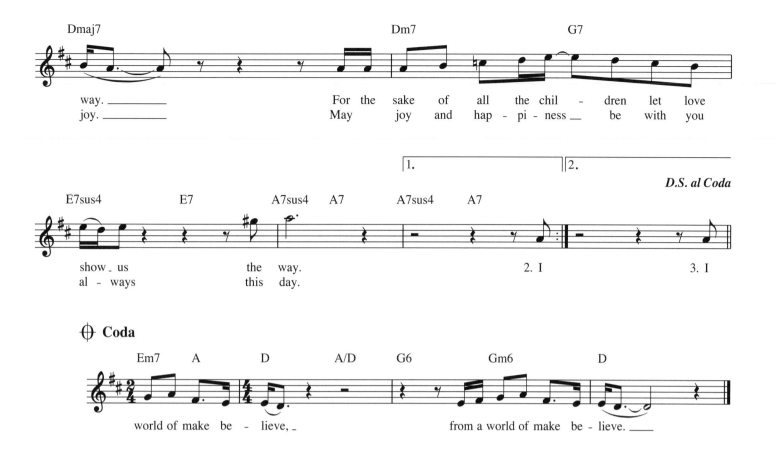

I'm Spending Christmas with You

Words and Music by Tom Occhipinti

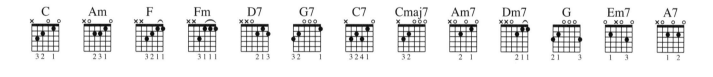

Strum Pattern: 7
Pick Pattern: 7

Verse
Moderately slow

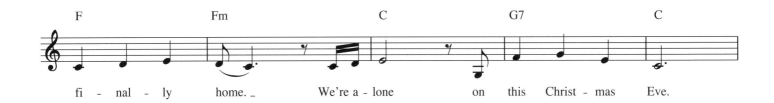

fi - nal - ly home. _ We're a - lone on this Christ - mas Eve.

%% **Chorus**

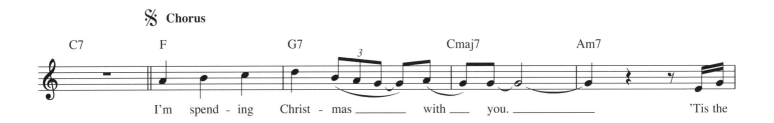

I'm spend - ing Christ - mas _____ with _____ you. _____ 'Tis the

sea - son _____ when love is re - newed. _____ My hol - i - day

To Coda ⊕

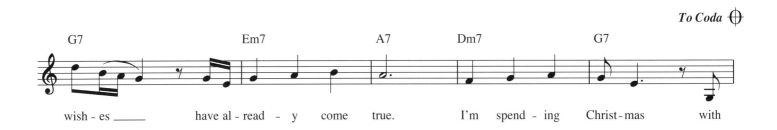

wish - es _____ have al - read - y come true. I'm spend - ing Christ - mas with

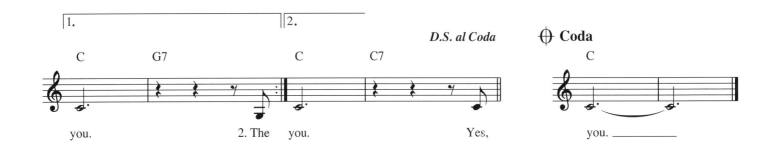

|1.

you.

2. The you.

Yes,

|2.

D.S. al Coda   ⊕ **Coda**

you. _____

Additional Lyrics

2. The fireplace is burning and your hands feel so warm.
   We're hanging popcorn on the tree.
   I take you in my arms, your lips touch mine.
   It feels like our first Christmas Eve.

I'll Be Home for Christmas

Words and Music by Kim Gannon and Walter Kent

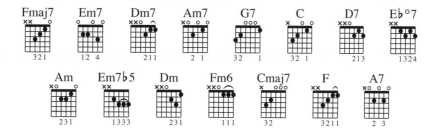

Strum Pattern: 4, 3
Pick Pattern: 4, 3

I'll Be Home on Christmas Day

Words and Music by Michael Jarrett

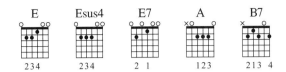

Strum Pattern: 3
Pick Pattern: 3

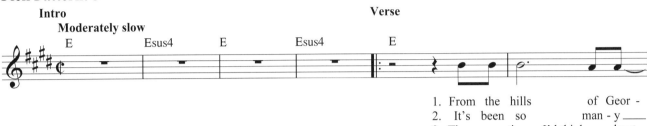

Intro

Moderately slow

Verse

1. From the hills of Geor -
2. It's been so man - y ___
3. There were times I'd think a - bout ___

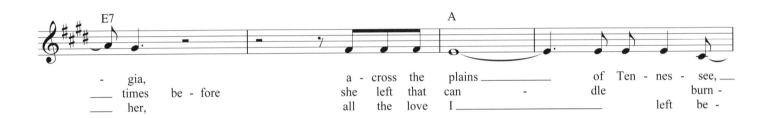

- gia, a - cross the plains ___ of Ten - nes - see,
___ times be - fore she left that can - dle burn -
___ her, all the love I ___ left be -

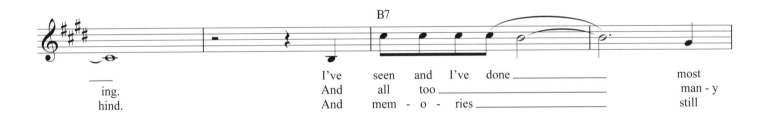

ing. I've seen and I've done ___ most
hind. And mem - o - ries ___ still

ev - 'ry - thing that a man can ___ do or
tears that fell, my soul ___ filled with
lin - ger with - in my ___ trou - bled

see. But if I ___ could on - ly
yearn - ing. If I had ___ an - y sense
mind. If I could ___ set a - side

I've Got My Love to Keep Me Warm

from the 20th Century Fox Motion Picture ON THE AVENUE
Words and Music by Irving Berlin

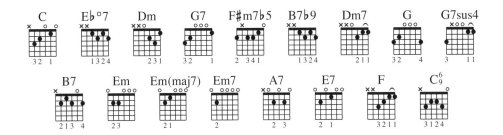

Strum Pattern: 3, 4
Pick Pattern: 3, 4

Verse

Brightly

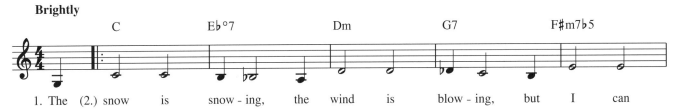

1. The (2.) snow is snow - ing, the wind is blow - ing, but I can

weath - er the storm. ___ What do I care how much it may storm?

___ I've got my love to keep me warm.

I can't re - mem - ber a worse De - cem - ber; just

watch those i - ci - cles form. _____ What do I care if

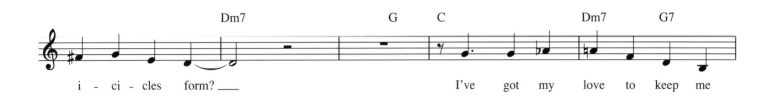

i - ci - cles form? ___ I've got my love to keep me

Bridge

warm. Off with my o - ver - coat, _ off with my

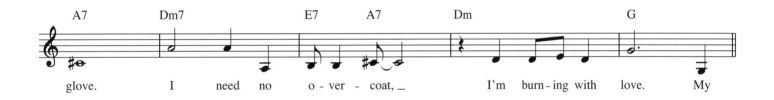

glove. I need no o - ver - coat, _ I'm burn - ing with love. My

Outro-Verse

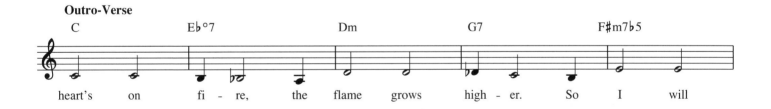

heart's on fi - re, the flame grows high - er. So I will

weath - er the storm. ___ What do I care how much it may storm? ___

I've got my love to keep me warm. 2. The warm. _____

It Must Have Been the Mistletoe
(Our First Christmas)

Words and Music by Justin Wilde and Doug Konecky

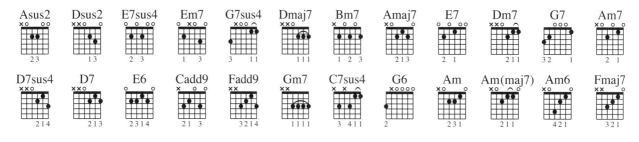

Strum Pattern: 8
Pick Pattern: 8

Verse

Moderately

1. It must have been _ the mis-tle-toe, _ the la-zy fire, _ the fall-ing snow, _ the

mag-ic in ____ the frost-y air, ____ that feel-ing ev-'ry-where. It

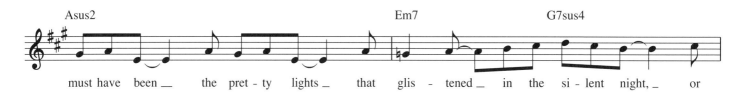

must have been _ the pret-ty lights _ that glis-tened _ in the si-lent night, _ or

may-be just ____ the stars so bright _ that shined a - bove you.

Bridge

Our first Christ - mas, more than _ we'd been dream - ing of. _

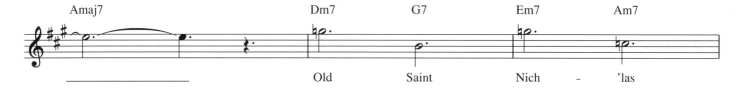

_____ Old Saint Nich - 'las

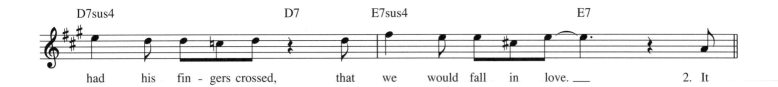

had his fin - gers crossed, that we would fall in love. ___ 2. It

Verse

could have been __ the hol - i - day, __ the mid-night ride __ up - on a sleigh, __ the

coun - try - side __ all dressed in white, _ that cra - zy snow - ball fight. It

could have been __ the stee - ple bell __ that wrapped us up with - in it's spell. __ It

on - ly took one kiss to know, __ it must have been the

Bridge

mis - tle - toe. Our first Christ - mas,

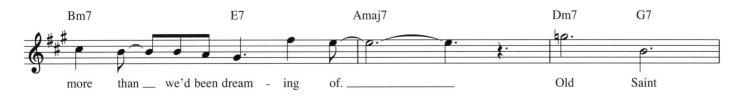

more than __ we'd been dream - ing of. _____ Old Saint

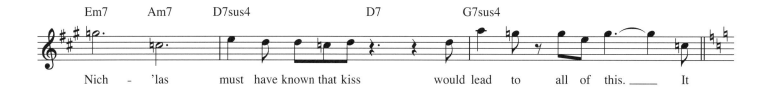

Em7   Am7   D7sus4   D7   G7sus4

Nich - 'las   must have known that kiss   would lead   to   all of this. _____ It

Outro

Cadd9

must have been __   the mis - tle - toe, ___   the la - zy fire, ___   the fall - ing snow, _   the

Fadd9   G7sus4

mag - ic in _____   the frost - y air, _____   that   made   me   love   you.   On

Cadd9   Gm7   C7sus4

Christ - mas Eve ___   a wish come true, __   that night I _____ fell in love with you. __   It

Fadd9   Dm7   G7sus4

on - ly took ___   one kiss to know, _   it   must have been   the

Cadd9   Dm7   G6   Am   Am(maj7) Am7   Am6

mis - tle - toe!   It must have been   the mis - tle - toe!   It

Dm7   G7sus4   Cadd9   Fmaj7   Cadd9

must have been   the mis - tle - toe!

It's Christmas Time All Over the World

Words and Music by Hugh Martin

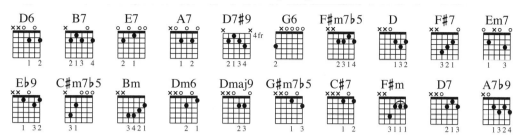

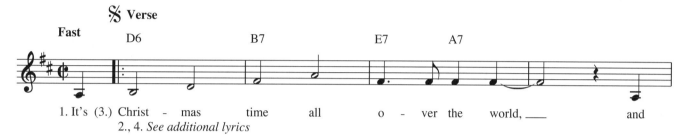

Strum Pattern: 4
Pick Pattern: 3

𝄋 **Verse**

Fast

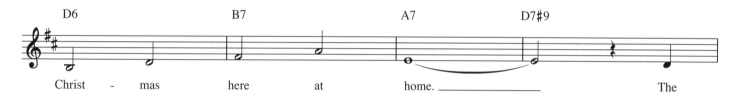

D6   B7   E7   A7

1. It's (3.) Christ - mas time all o - ver the world, ____ and
2., 4. *See additional lyrics*

D6   B7   A7   D7#9

Christ - mas here at home. _____ The

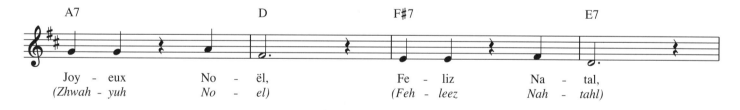

G6   E7   F#m7b5   B7

church bells chime wher - ev - er we roam, ____ so

A7   D   F#7   E7

Joy - eux No - ël,   Fe - liz Na - tal,
(Zhwah - yuh No - el)   (Feh - leez Nah - tahl)

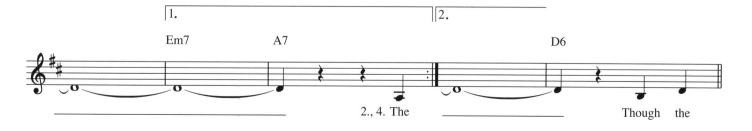

G6   Em7   Eb9   D

Gel - luk - kig Kerst - feest   to you! ____
(Huh - lukh - kuh Kairst - feest)

1.   2.

Em7   A7   D6

_____   2., 4. The   Though the

Bridge

cus - toms _____ may change, _____ and the lan - guage _____

_____ is strange, _____ this ap - peal we feel is

real in Hol - land or Hong _____ Kong. _____ It's

Outro

Christ - mas time all o - ver the world, _____ in

plac - es near and far; _____ and so, my

friends, wher - ev - er you are, _____ a Fröh - li - che Weih -
(Fruh - lee - kheh Vy -

nacht - en! Ka - la Christ - ou - ge - na! Yo - i Kurisu -
nakh - ten) (Kah - lah Hrees - too - yeh-nah) (Yo - ee Kreess -

ma - su! Which means a ver - y mer - ry Christ - mas
mah - soo)

to you! _____ 3. It's

Coda

Christ - mas _____ to

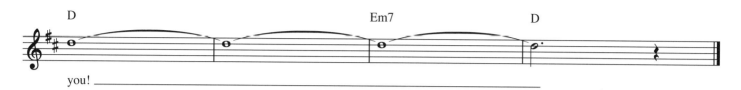

you! _____

Additional Lyrics

2., 4. The snow is thick in most of the world
And children's eyes are wide
As old Saint Nick gets ready to ride,
So Feliz Navidad, Crăciun Fericit,
(Feh-lees Nah-vee-dahd) (Krah-choon Feeh-ree-cheet)
And Happy New Year to you!

Jesus Is Born

Words and Music by Steve Green, Phil Naish and Colleen Green

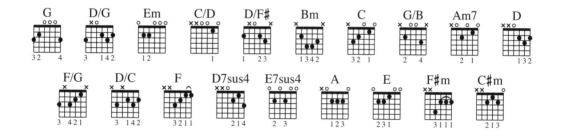

*Strum Pattern: 2
*Pick Pattern: 4

Intro

Moderately fast

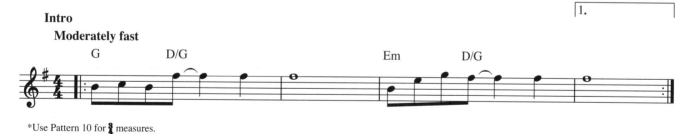

*Use Pattern 10 for ⅞ measures.

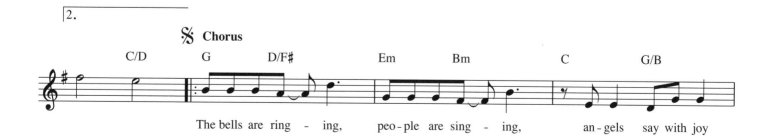

The bells are ring - ing, peo-ple are sing - ing, an - gels say with joy

4th time, To Coda ⊕

"Je - sus is born!" There in a man - ger, He was no stran - ger. Pro-phe-sied, now a - live,

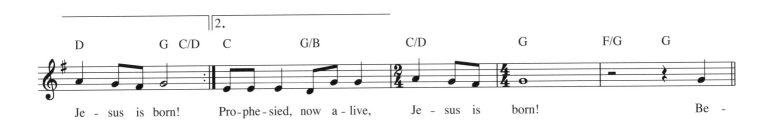

Je - sus is born! Pro-phe-sied, now a - live, Je - sus is born! Be -

Bridge

hold the gift of sal - va - tion, a light for ___ all to see, re -

veal - ing all God's glo - ry, Em - man - u - el is He. _____ Be -

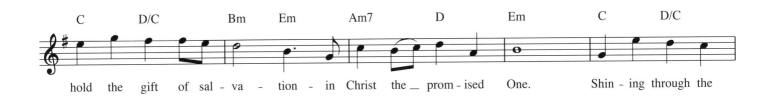

hold the gift of sal - va - tion in Christ the ___ prom - ised One. Shin - ing through the

D.S. al Coda
(take repeat)

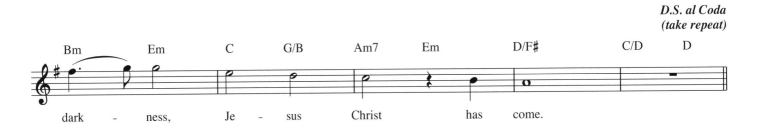

dark - ness, Je - sus Christ has come.

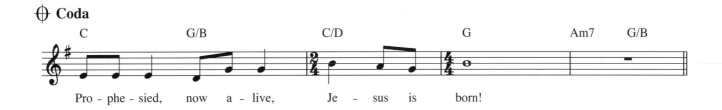

Coda

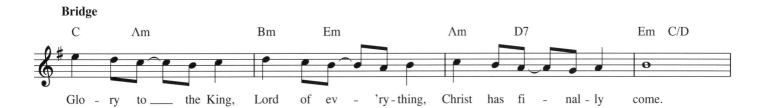

Pro - phe - sied, now a - live, Je - sus is born!

Bridge

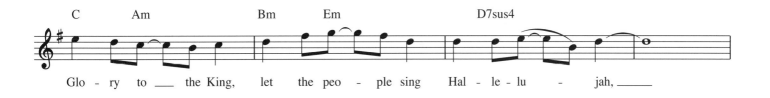

Glo - ry to ___ the King, Lord of ev - 'ry - thing, Christ has fi - nal - ly come.

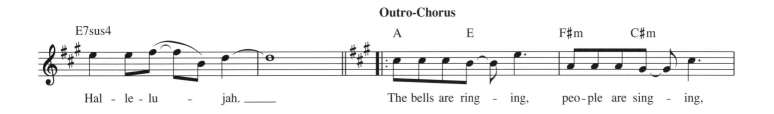

Glo - ry to ___ the King, let the peo - ple sing Hal - le - lu - jah, _____

Outro-Chorus

Hal - le - lu - jah. _____ The bells are ring - ing, peo - ple are sing - ing,

an - gels say with joy, "Je - sus is born!" There in a man - ger, He was no stran - ger.

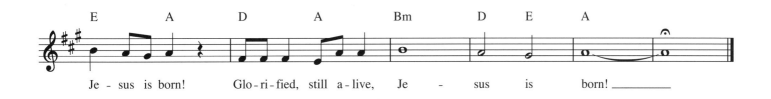

Glo - ri - fied, still a - live, Je - sus is born! Je - sus is born! Glo - ri - fied, still a - live,

Je - sus is born! Glo - ri - fied, still a - live, Je - sus is born! _____

It Won't Seem Like Christmas
(Without You)

Words and Music by J.A. Balthrop

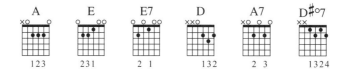

Strum Pattern: 9
Pick Pattern: 7

Oh, it

won't   seem   like   Christ - mas,   oh,   with - out   you,   for

too   man - y   miles ___   are   be - tween.   But   if

I _____   get   the   one   thing ___   that   I'm   wish - ing   for ___   then   I'll ___

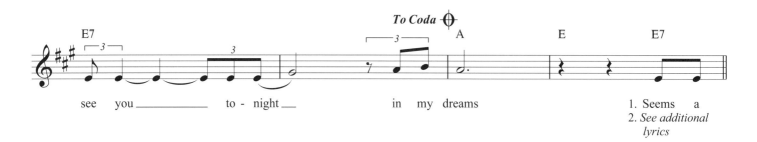

see   you _____   to - night ___   in   my   dreams

1. Seems   a
2. *See additional lyrics*

Verse

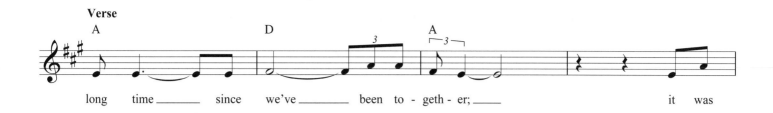

long time _____ since we've _____ been to - geth - er; _____ it was

just a - bout _____ to this time of year. _____ Looks like

it's _____ gon - na be _____ snow - y wea - ther. _____ How I

wish that you could be here. _____ But it

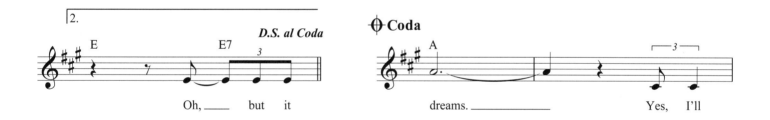

Oh, _____ but it

Coda

dreams. _____ Yes, I'll

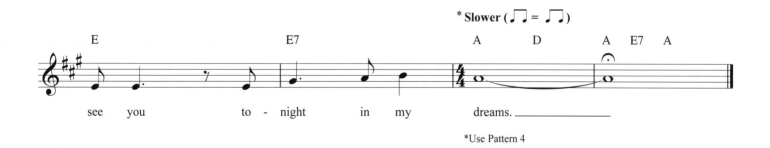

see you to - night in my dreams. _____

*Use Pattern 4

Additional Lyrics

2. In the distance I hear sleigh bells ringing.
The holly's so pretty this year;
And the carol that somebody's singing
Reminds me of our Christmas last year.

It's Beginning to Look Like Christmas

By Meredith Willson

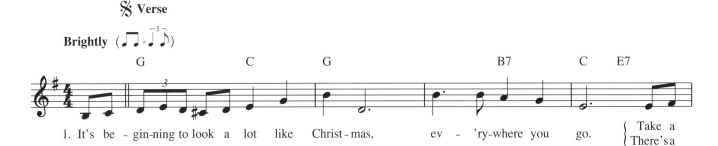

Strum Pattern: 2, 3
Pick Pattern: 3, 4

% Verse

Brightly

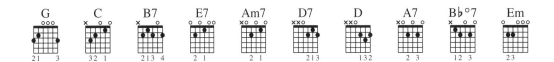

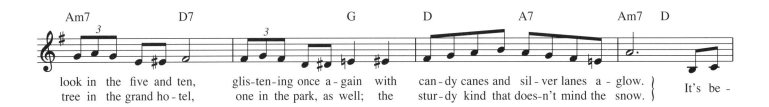

1. It's be - gin-ning to look a lot like Christ-mas, ev - 'ry-where you go. Take a / There's a

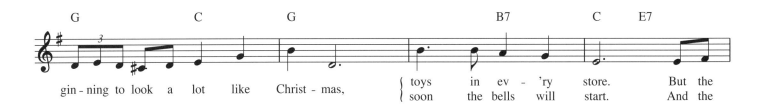

look in the five and ten, glis-ten-ing once a - gain with can - dy canes and sil - ver lanes a - glow. / It's be -
tree in the grand ho - tel, one in the park, as well; the stur - dy kind that does-n't mind the snow. /

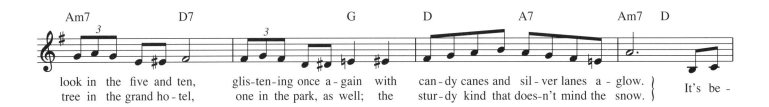

gin - ning to look a lot like Christ - mas, toys in ev - 'ry store. But the
soon the bells will start. And the

To Coda

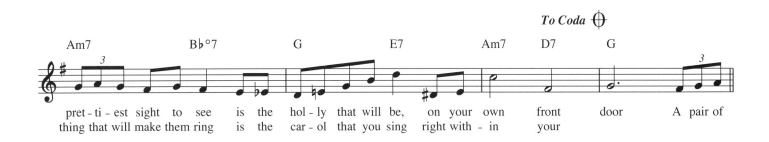

pret - ti - est sight to see is the hol - ly that will be, on your own front door A pair of
thing that will make them ring is the car - ol that you sing right with - in your

Bridge

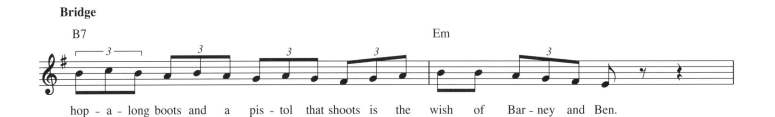

hop - a - long boots and a pis - tol that shoots is the wish of Bar - ney and Ben.

Dolls that will talk and will go for a walk is the hope of Jan-ice and Jen. And

D.S. al Coda

Mom and Dad can hard-ly wait for school to start a-gain. 2. It's be-

heart.

Jingle Bell Rock

Words and Music by Joe Beal and Jim Boothe

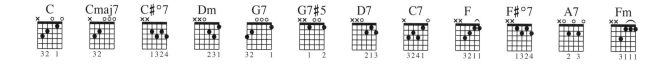

Strum Pattern: 1, 3
Pick Pattern: 2, 3

Verse
Moderate Rock

1., 2. Jin-gle-bell, jin-gle-bell, jin-gle-bell rock, jin-gle-bell swing and jin-gle-bells ring.

Snow-in' and blow-in' up bush-els of fun, now the jin-gle-hop has be-gun.

Jin-gle-bell, jin-gle-bell, jin-gle-bell rock, jin-gle-bells chime in jin-gle-bell time.

Dan - cin' and pran - cin' in Jin - gle - bell Square in the frost - y air. What a

Bridge

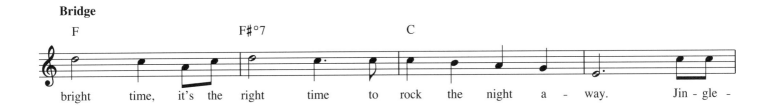

bright time, it's the right time to rock the night a - way. Jin - gle -

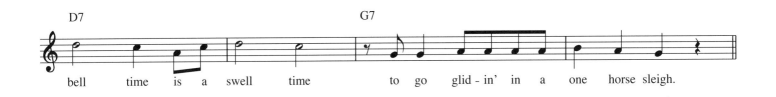

bell time is a swell time to go glid - in' in a one horse sleigh.

Outro

Gid - dy - up, jin - gle horse pick up your feet, jin - gle a - round the clock.

1.

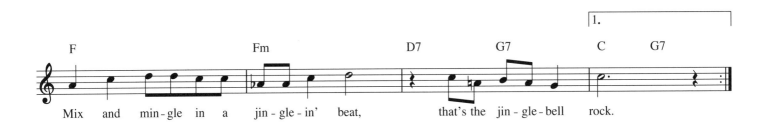

Mix and min - gle in a jin - gle - in' beat, that's the jin - gle - bell rock.

2.

that's the jin - gle - bell, that's the jin - gle - bell rock. _____

The Last Month of the Year
(What Month Was Jesus Born In?)

Words and Music by Vera Hall
Adapted and Arranged by Ruby Pickens Tartt and Alan Lomax

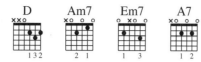

Strum Pattern: 6
Pick Pattern: 3

Verse

Moderately

1. What month _ was my Je - sus born _ in? Last month _ of the year!
2., 3., 4 *See additional lyrics*

What month _ was my Je - sus born _ in? Last month _ of the year! _ Oh,

Chorus

Jan - u - ar - y, Feb - ru - ar - y, March, _____

A - pril, May, June, O Lord, _ You got Ju - ly, Au - gust, Sep - tem - ber, Oc -

to - ber and a No - vem - ber, on the twen - ty fifth day of De - cem - ber in the

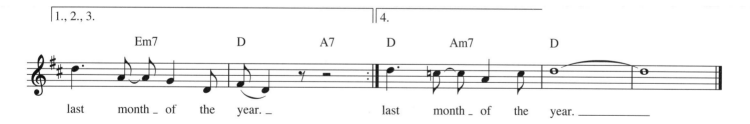

1., 2., 3. last month _ of the year. _   *4.* last month _ of the year. _____

Additional Lyrics

2. Well, they laid Him in the manger,
   Last month of the year!
   Well, they laid Him in the manger,
   Last month of the year!

3. Wrapped Him up in swaddling clothing,
   Last month of the year!
   Wrapped Him up in swaddling clothing,
   Last month of the year!

4. He was born of the Virgin Mary,
   Last month of the year!
   He was born of the Virgin Mary,
   Last month of the year!

It's Christmas in New York

Words and Music by Billy Butt

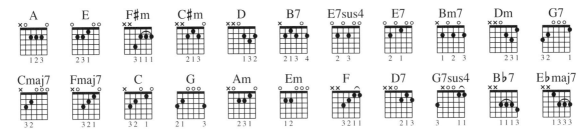

Strum Pattern: 4
Pick Pattern: 3

Verse

Moderately

1., 2. Church-bells are ring-ing, __ choirs __ are sing-ing, __

joy they are bring-ing, __ it's Christ-mas in New York.

Street-lights are pleas-ing, __ snow-flakes are teas-ing, __

Cen-tral Park's freez-ing, __ it's Christ-mas in ____ New __ York. The

Bridge

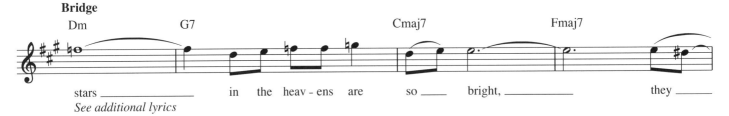

stars ____ in the heav-ens are so __ bright, ____ they ____

See additional lyrics

____ tell ____ of a ba-by that was born ____ on this night.

Verse

3. Stock-ings are fill-ing, __ cham-pagne is chill-ing, __

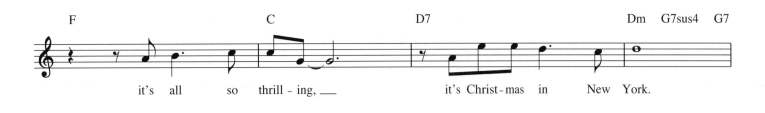

it's all so thrill - ing, __ it's Christ - mas in New York.

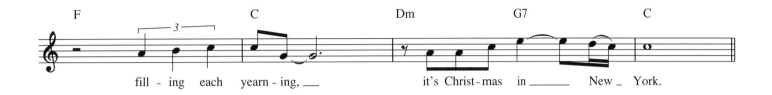

Log fires are burn - ing, __ San - ta's re - turn - ing __

fill - ing each yearn - ing, __ it's Christ - mas in _____ New _ York.

Interlude

Outro

Church - bells are ring - ing, choirs __ are sing - ing, _____

__ joy _____ they are bring - ing, __ it's Christ - mas in New York,

it's Christ - mas in New York, it's Christ - mas in New York. __

Additional Lyrics

2. Rest'rant signs swaying, blue skies are graying,
Ev'ryone saying, it's Christmas in New York.
Skyscrapers gleaming, Broadway lights beaming,
Children are dreaming, it's Christmas in New York.

Bridge The lights on the Christmas tree are fine,
The sights of shopping sprees, the gifts, yours and mine.

Jingle, Jingle, Jingle

Music and Lyrics by Johnny Marks

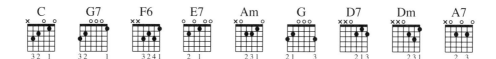

Strum Pattern: 4
Pick Pattern: 4

Verse
Moderately

1., 2. Jin - gle, jin - gle, jin - gle, you will hear {my / his} sleigh bells ring.

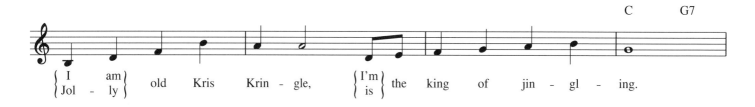

{I am / Jol - ly} old Kris Krin - gle, {I'm / is} the king of jin - gl - ing.

Jin - gle, jin - gle rein - deer, through the frost - y air they'll go.

They are not just plain deer, they're the fast - est deer I know. You
Spoken: (Ho! Ho!)

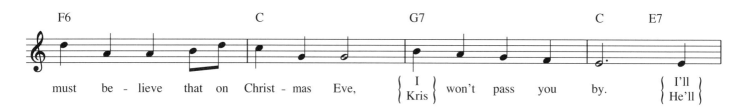

must be - lieve that on Christ - mas Eve, {I / Kris} won't pass you by. {I'll / He'll}

dash a - way in {my / his} mag - ic sleigh, fly - ing through the sky.

Jin - gle, jin - gle rein - deer, through the frost - y air they'll go.

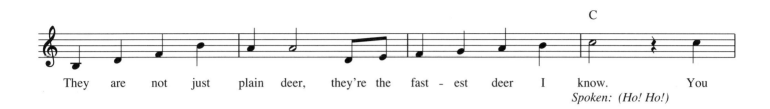

They are not just plain deer, they're the fast - est deer I know. You

Spoken: (Ho! Ho!)

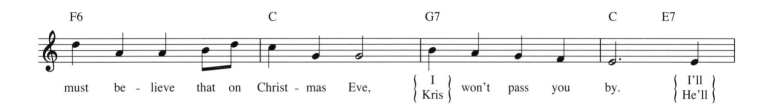

must be - lieve that on Christ - mas Eve, { I / Kris } won't pass you by. { I'll / He'll }

dash a - way in { my / his } mag - ic sleigh, fly - ing through the sky.

Jin - gle, jin - gle, jin - gle, you will hear { my / his } sleigh bells ring.

1.

{ I am old Kris Krin - gle; I'm the king of jin - gl - ing. / Jol - ly old Kris Krin - gle is the }

Spoken: (Ho! Ho!)

2.

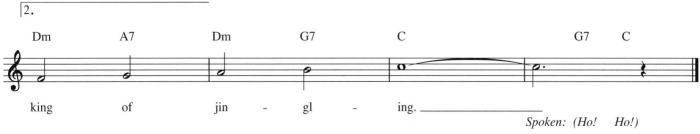

king of jin - gl - ing. ___

Spoken: (Ho! Ho!)

Let It Snow! Let It Snow! Let It Snow!

Words by Sammy Cahn
Music by Jule Styne

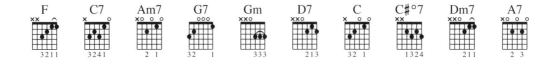

Strum Pattern: 2
Pick Pattern: 4

A Marshmallow World

Words by Carl Sigman
Music by Peter De Rose

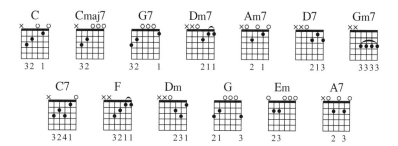

Strum Pattern: 3
Pick Pattern: 3

Intro
Brightly

1. It's a

%̸ Verse

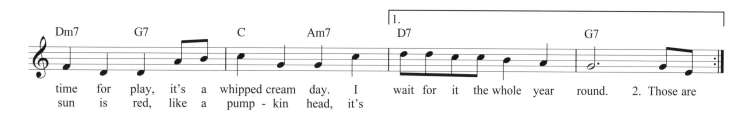

(4.) marsh-mal-low world in the win-ter when the snow comes to cov-er the ground. It's the
marsh-mal-low clouds be-ing friend-ly in the arms of ev-er-green trees. And the

time for play, it's a whipped cream day. I wait for it the whole year round. 2. Those are
sun is red, like a pump-kin head, it's

shin-ing so your nose won't freeze. The world is your snow ball; see how it grows.

That's how it goes, when-ev-er it snows. The world is your snow ball; just for a song, get

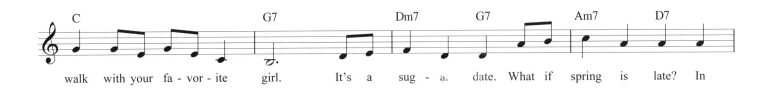

Merry Christmas, Baby

Words and Music by Lou Baxter and Johnny Moore

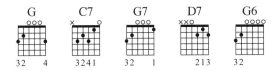

Strum Pattern: 1, 3
Pick Pattern: 4, 5

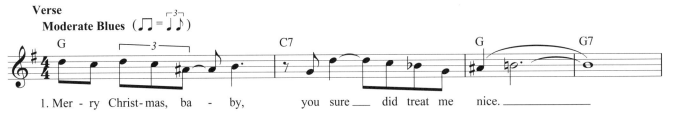

The Little Boy That Santa Claus Forgot

Words and Music by Michael Carr, Tommy Connor and Jimmy Leach

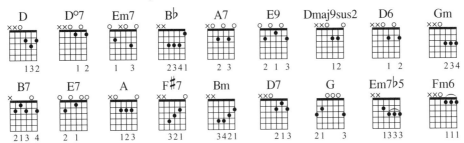

Strum Pattern: 4
Pick Pattern: 3

Intro
Slowly

Verse

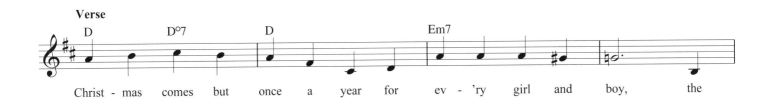

Christ - mas comes but once a year for ev - 'ry girl and boy, the

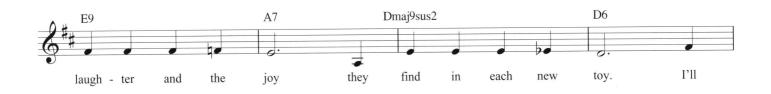

laugh - ter and the joy they find in each new toy. I'll

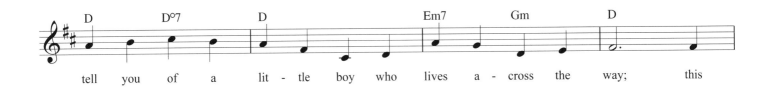

tell you of a lit - tle boy who lives a - cross the way; this

lit - tle fel - ler's Christ - mas is just an - oth - er day. He's the

Chorus

lit - tle boy that San - ta Claus for - got, _____ and good - ness knows he did - n't want a lot. _____ He sent a note to San - ta for some sol - diers and a drum; it broke his lit - tle heart when he found San - ta had - n't come. In the street he en - vies all those luck - y boys, _____ then wan - ders home to last year's bro - ken toys. _____ I'm so sor - ry for that lad - die, he has - n't got a dad - dy, the lit - tle boy that San - ta Claus for -

got. He's the got. _____

The Little Drummer Boy

**Words and Music by Harry Simeone,
Henry Onorati and Katherine Davis**

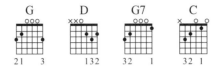

Strum Pattern: 3
Pick Pattern:

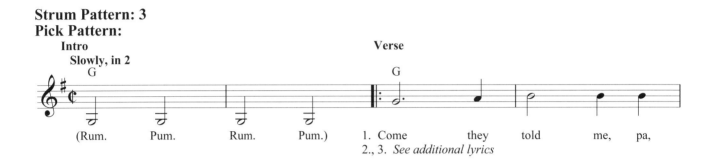

(Rum. Pum. Rum. Pum.) 1. Come they told me, pa,
2., 3. *See additional lyrics*

rum, pum, pum, pum. (Rum. Pum. Rum.) A new-born King to see, pa,

rum, pum, pum, pum. (Rum. Pum. Rum.) Our fin-est gifts we bring, pa,

rum, pum, pum, pum, (Rum. Pum. Rum.) to lay be-fore the King, pa,

rum, pum, pum, pum, rum, pum, pum, pum, rum, pum, pum, pum. (Rum. Pum.)

So to hon-or Him, pa, rum, pum, pum, pum, (Rum. Pum.)

when _ we come. (Rum. Pum. Rum. Pum. Pum. Rum. Pum. Pum.)

Then He smiled at me, pa, rum, pum, pum, pum, (Rum. Pum.)

me and my drum. (Rum. Pum. Rum. Pum. Pum. Rum. Pum. Pum.)

Outro

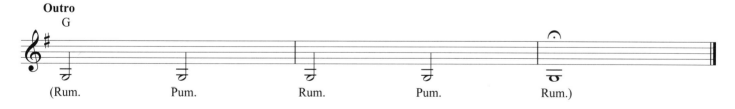

(Rum. Pum. Rum. Pum. Rum.)

Additional Lyrics

2. Baby Jesus, pa, rum, pum, pum, pum,
   I am a poor boy too, pa, rum, pum, pum, pum.
   I have no gift to bring, pa, rum, pum, pum, pum.
   That's fit to give our King, pa, rum, pum, pum, pum,
   Rum, pum, pum, pum, rum, pum, pum, pum.
   Shall I play for You, pa, rum, pum, pum, pum,
   On my drum?

3. Mary nodded, pa, rum, pum, pum, pum,
   The ox and lamb kept time, pa, rum, pum, pum, pum.
   I played my drum for Him, pa, rum, pum, pum, pum.
   I played my best for Him, pa, rum, pum, pum, pum,
   Rum, pum, pum, rum, pum, pum, pum.
   Then He smiled at me, pa, rum, pum, pum, pum,
   Me and my drum.

Little Saint Nick

Words and Music by Brian Wilson and Mike Love

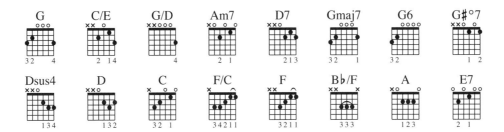

Strum Pattern: 1, 3
Pick Pattern: 4, 5

Intro
Moderately fast (♪♪ = ♪ ♪)

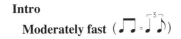

G C/E G/D C/E G C/E G/D C/E   Am7   D7

Ooh,   mer - ry   Christ - mas

G   Am7   D7

Saint   Nick. _____   Ooh. _____   1. Well, __
(Christ - mas comes this time each   year.) __

Verse

Am7   D7   Am   D7   G   Gmaj7

way   up north where the   air gets   cold, __ there's a tale a - bout Christ - mas that you've
2., 3. *See additional lyrics*

G6   G#°7   Am7   D7   Am7   D7

all been told. __ And a   real fa - mous cat   all dressed up in   red, __   and he

Chorus

G   Gmaj7   G6   C

spends the whole __ year work - in' out on his sled. __   It's the   Lit - tle Saint Nick. (Lit - tle

To Coda ⊕

Am7   Dsus4   D |1.   Dsus4   D |2.

Saint Nick.) It's the Lit - tle Saint Nick. (Lit - tle Saint Nick.) 2. Just a Saint Nick.)

Bridge

C   F/C   C   F   Bb/F   F

Run, run, rein - deer. _____ Run, run, rein - deer. Oh. _____

C   F/C   C   A   N.C.

Run, run, rein - deer. _____ Run, run, rein - deer. He don't miss no one. 3. And

⊕ **Coda**

Outro

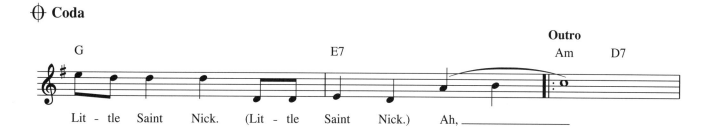

G   E7   Am   D7

Lit - tle Saint Nick. (Lit - tle Saint Nick.) Ah, _____

Repeat and fade

Am7   D7   G   E7

mer - ry Christ - mas Saint Nick. _____   Ah, _____
             (Christ - mas comes this time each year.) _____

Additional Lyrics

2. Just a little bobsled, we call it Old Saint Nick,
   But she'll walk a toboggan with a four-speed stick.
   She's candy-apple red with a ski for a wheel,
   And when Santa hits the gas, man, just watch her peel.

3. And haulin' through the snow at a fright'nin' speed
   With a half a dozen deer with Rudy to lead.
   He's gotta wear his goggles 'cause the snow really flies,
   And he's cruisin' ev'ry pad with a little surprise.

101

Mary, Did You Know?

Words and Music by Mark Lowry and Buddy Greene

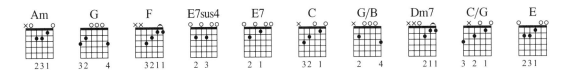

Strum Pattern: 6
Pick Pattern: 4

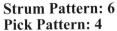

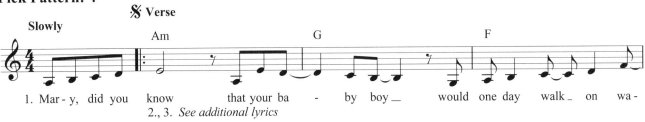

1. Mar-y, did you know that your ba - by boy would one day walk on wa-
2., 3. *See additional lyrics*

-ter? Mar-y, did you know that your ba - by boy would save our sons and daugh-

-ters? Did you know that your ba - by boy has come to make you new?

This child that you de - liv - ered will soon de - liv - er you?

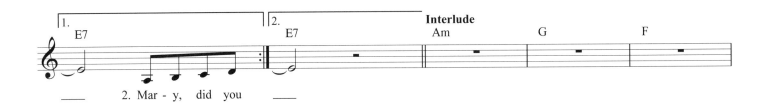

2. Mar-y, did you

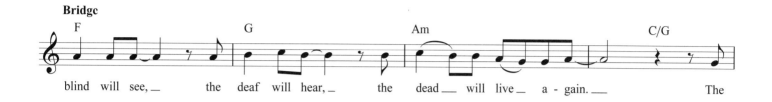

Bridge

blind will see, __ the deaf will hear, __ the dead __ will live __ a - gain. __ The

lame will leap, __ the dumb will speak __ the prais - es of __ the lamb. __

Coda

Outro

2nd time, vocal tacet

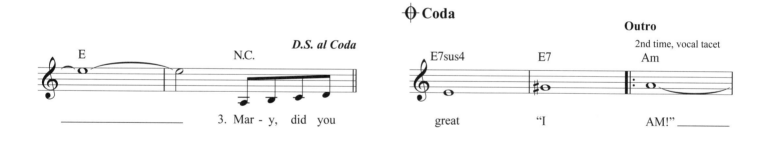

D.S. al Coda

_____ 3. Mar - y, did you   great   "I   AM!" _____

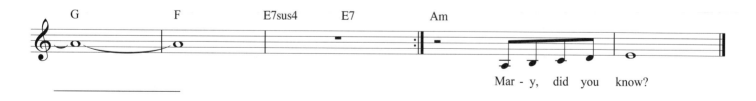

Mar - y, did you know?

Additional Lyrics

2. Mary, did you know that your baby boy will give sight to the blind man?
   Mary, did you know that your baby boy would calm a storm with his hand?
   Did you know that your baby boy has walked where angels trod,
   When you kiss your little baby, you've kissed the face of God?

3. Mary, did you know that your baby boy is Lord of all creation?
   Mary, did you know that your baby boy would one day rule the nations?
   Did you know that your baby boy was heaven's perfect lamb?
   That the sleeping Child you're holding is the great "I AM!"

Merry Christmas, Darling

Words and Music by Richard Carpenter and Frank Pooler

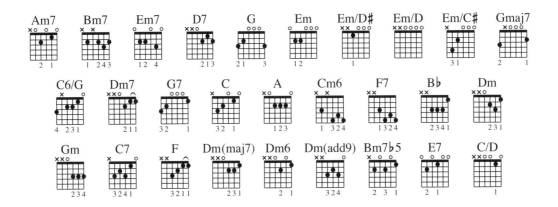

Strum Pattern: 4
Pick Pattern: 4

Intro
Freely

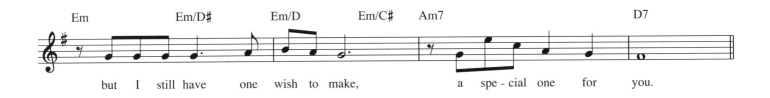

Greet-ing cards have all been sent, the Christ-mas rush is through,

*Let chords ring throughout Intro

but I still have one wish to make, a spe-cial one for you.

Verse
Moderately slow

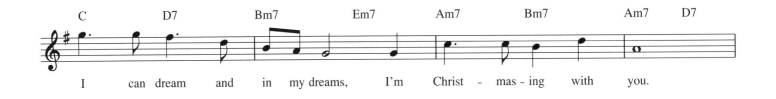

Mer-ry Christ-mas, dar-ling, We're a-part, that's true; but
I can dream and in my dreams, I'm Christ-mas-ing with you.

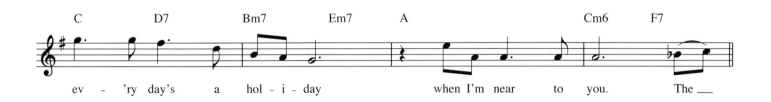

Hol - i - days are joy - ful, there's al - ways some - thing new. But

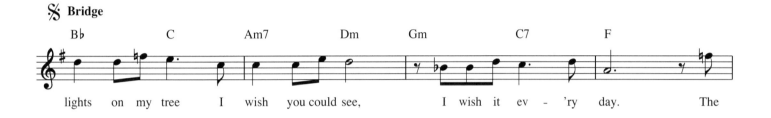

ev - 'ry day's a hol - i - day when I'm near to you. The ___

Bridge

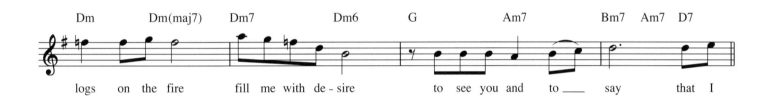

lights on my tree I wish you could see, I wish it ev - 'ry day. The

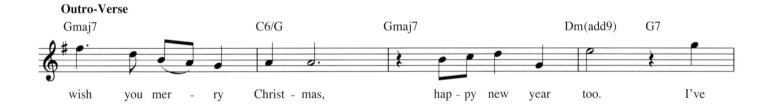

logs on the fire fill me with de - sire to see you and to ___ say that I

Outro-Verse

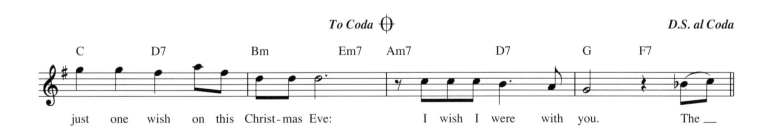

wish you mer - ry Christ - mas, hap - py new year too. I've

To Coda ⊕   *D.S. al Coda*

just one wish on this Christ - mas Eve: I wish I were with you. The ___

⊕ **Coda**

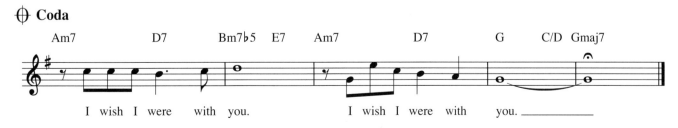

I wish I were with you. I wish I were with you. _____

The Merry Christmas Polka

Words by Paul Francis Webster
Music by Sonny Burke

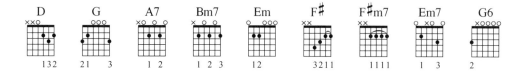

Strum Pattern: 4
Pick Pattern: 3

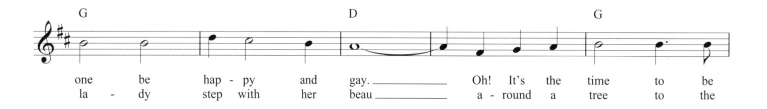

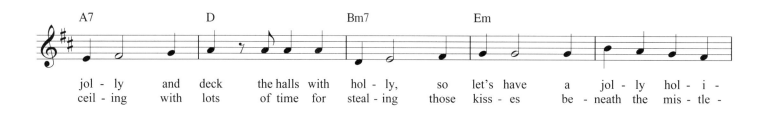

an - oth - er joy - ous sea - son has be - gun. Roll out the
with ev - 'ry - bod - y join - ing in the fun. Roll out the

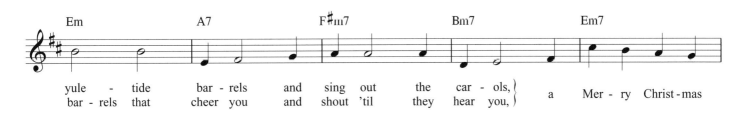

yule - tide bar - rels and sing out the car - ols,} a Mer - ry Christ - mas
bar - rels that cheer you and shout 'til they hear you,}

ev - 'ry - one! 2. Come on and one!___

Mister Santa

Words and Music by Pat Ballard

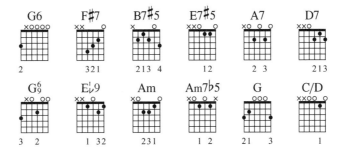

Strum Pattern: 4
Pick Pattern: 3

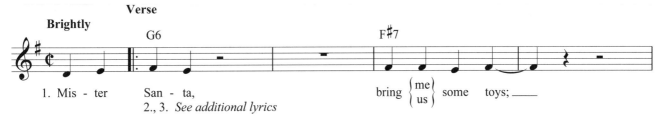

1. Mis - ter San - ta, bring {me us} some toys;___
2., 3. *See additional lyrics*

bring Mer - ry Christ - mas to all girls and boys,___

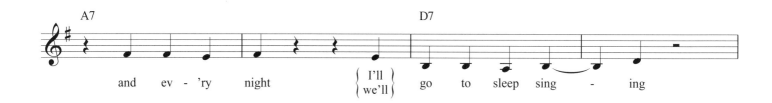

and ev - 'ry night { I'll / we'll } go to sleep sing - ing

and dream a - bout the pres - ents you'll be bring - ing.

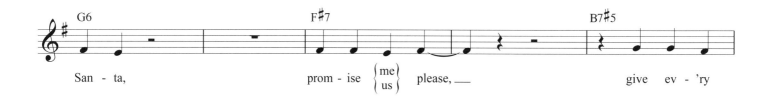

San - ta, prom - ise { me / us } please, ___ give ev - 'ry

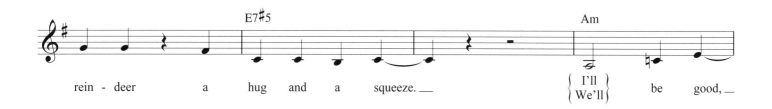

rein - deer a hug and a squeeze. ___ { I'll / We'll } be good, ___

___ as good can be, ___ Mis - ter San - ta

don't for - get me. ___ 2., 3. Mis - ter _____

Additional Lyrics

2. Mister Santa, dear old Saint Nick
   Be awful careful and please don't get sick.
   Put on your coat when breezes are blowin'
   And when you cross the street look where you're goin'.
   Santa, we (I) love you so,
   We (I) hope you never get lost in the snow.
   Take your time when you unpack,
   Mister Santa don't hurry back.

3. Mister Santa, we've been so good.
   We've washed the dishes and done what we should.
   Made up the beds and scrubbed up our toesies.
   We've used a kleenex when we've blown our nosesies.
   Santa look at our ears, they're clean as whistles.
   We're sharper than shears.
   Now we've put you on the spot,
   Mister Santa bring us a lot.

Merry Christmas Waltz

Words and Music by Bob Batson and Inez Loewer

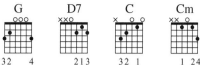

Strum Pattern: 8, 9
Pick Pattern: 7, 8

Intro
Moderate waltz

Verse

1. While we're (2.)waltz - in', while we're

{ dream - ing, } { dream - ing }
{ sing - ing, } ev - 'ry - one's { sing - ing } too. Mer - ry Christ - mas, mer - ry Christ - mas, mer - ry

Christ - mas to you. Bells are ring - in' _____ clear - er and clear - er, _____

bring - ing Christ - mas near - er and near - er. Mu - sic play - ing, cou - ples sway - ing, what a

beau - ti - ful sight, and the sea - son is the rea - son we're so hap - py to -

night. So stay in my arms, dar - ing, keep sing - in' _____ too. Mer - ry

1.
Christ - mas, mer - ry Christ - mas to you.

2.
2. While we're you. _____

Merry, Merry Christmas, Baby

Words and Music by Gilbert Lopez and Margo Sylvia

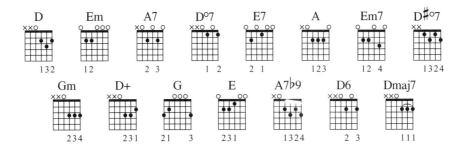

Strum Pattern: 7, 8
Pick Pattern: 7, 8

Intro
Slow Rock

1. Mer - ry, mer - ry Christ - mas ba - by. _____

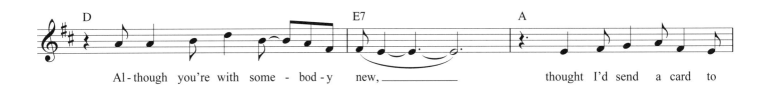

Al - though you're with some - bod - y new, _____ thought I'd send a card to

say that I wish this ___ hol - i - day would find me ___ be - side ___ you. _____

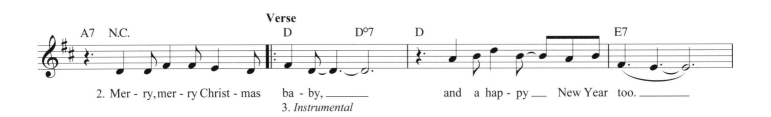

2. Mer - ry, mer - ry Christ - mas ba - by, _____ and a hap - py ___ New Year too. _____
3. *Instrumental*

It was Christ - mas Eve we met, a hol - i - day I ___ can't for - get, 'cause that's when we fell in

love. ___   I still ___ re - mem - ber ___ the gifts we gave ___ to each

Instrumental ends

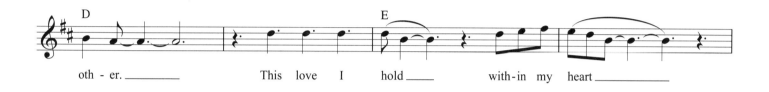

oth - er. ___ This love I hold ___ with - in my heart ___

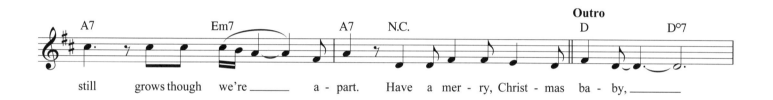

still grows though we're ___ a - part. Have a mer - ry, Christ - mas ba - by, ___

and a hap - py ___ New Year too. ___ I am hop - ing that you'll

find a ___ love as ___ true as mine. Mer - ry, mer - ry Christ - mas ba - by. ___

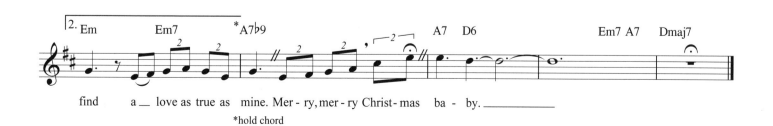

find a ___ love as true as mine. Mer - ry, mer - ry Christ - mas ba - by. ___

*hold chord

Miss You Most at Christmas Time

Words and Music by Mariah Carey and Walter Afanasieff

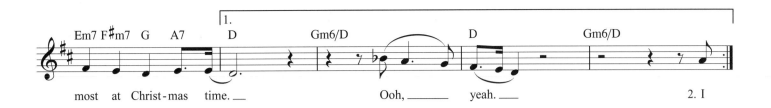

most at Christ-mas time. ___ Ooh, ___ yeah. ___ 2. I

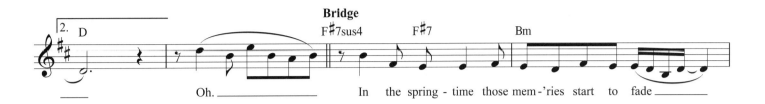

___ Oh. ___ In the spring-time those mem-'ries start to fade ___

with the A - pril rain. _____ Through the sum-mer days, _ till

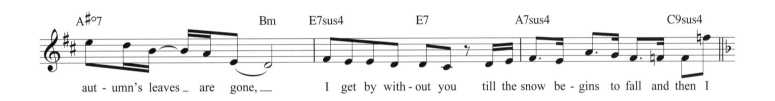

aut-umn's leaves _ are gone, _ I get by with-out you till the snow be-gins to fall and then I

Outro-Chorus

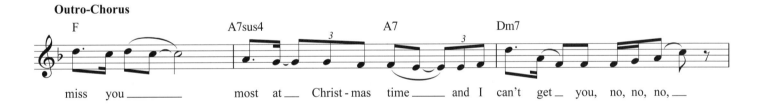

miss you ___ most at __ Christ-mas time ___ and I can't get _ you, no, no, no, __

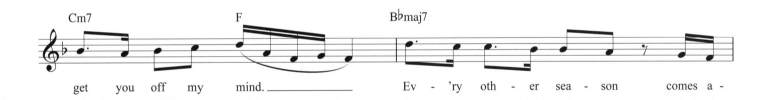

get you off my mind. _____ Ev - 'ry oth - er sea - son comes a -

long and I'm al-right. _____ But then I miss you most at Christ - mas _

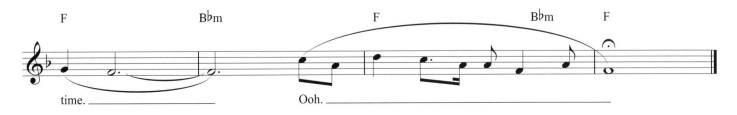

time. _____ Ooh. ___

The Most Wonderful Day of the Year

Music and Lyrics by Johnny Marks

Strum Pattern: 7
Pick Pattern: 7

here, _____ the most won-der-ful day of the year! _____ Toys

ga - lore _____ scat-tered on the floor. _____ There's no

room for more _____ and it's all be-cause of San - ta

Claus! A scoot-er for Jim-my, a dol-ly for Sue, the kind that will

e-ven say "How do ya do!" When Christ-mas Day is here. _____ The most

1.
won-der-ful day of the year. _____ 2. A won-der-ful, won-der-ful,

2.

won-der-ful, won-der-ful, won-der-ful day of _____ the year! _____

Additional Lyrics

Intro Up at the North Pole they have their laws,
Elves must work ev'ry day.
Making the toys that Old Santa Claus
Leads upon his sleigh.

Chorus When Christmas Day is here,
The most wonderful day of the year!
Spirits gay; ev'ryone will say, "Happy Holiday!
And the best to you all the whole year through."
An electric train hidden high on a shelf
That Daddy gives David but then runs himself.
When Christmas Day is here,
The most wonderful, wonderful, wonderful,
Wonderful, wonderful day of the year!

The Most Wonderful Time of the Year

Words and Music by Eddie Pola and George Wyle

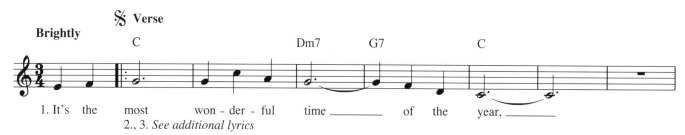

Strum Pattern: 7
Pick Pattern: 8

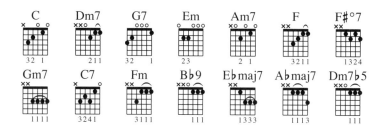

1. It's the most won-der-ful time of the year,
2., 3. *See additional lyrics*

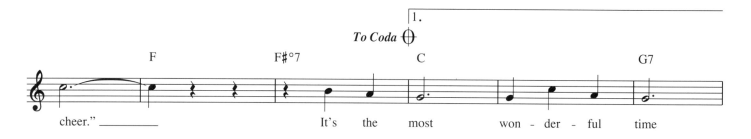

with the kids jin-gle bell-ing and ev-'ry-one tell-ing, "You be of good

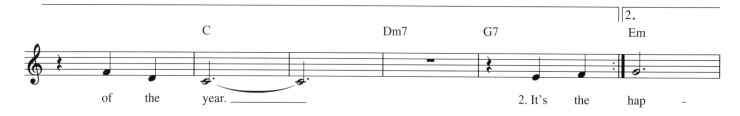

cheer." It's the most won-der-ful time

of the year. 2. It's the hap-

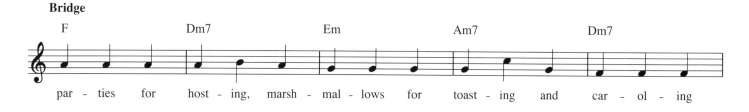

hap-pi-est sea - son of all. There'll be

Bridge

par-ties for host-ing, marsh-mal-lows for toast-ing and car-ol-ing

Additional Lyrics

2. It's the hap-happiest season of all,
With those holiday greetings
And gay happy meetings
When friends come to call.
It's the hap-happiest season of all.

3. It's the most wonderful time of the year.
There'll be much mistletoeing
And hearts will be glowing
When loved ones are near.
It's the most wonderful time of the year.

My Favorite Things

from THE SOUND OF MUSIC
Lyrics by Oscar Hammerstein II
Music by Richard Rodgers

Strum Pattern: 7
Pick Pattern: 8

Verse
Moderately

1. Rain - drops on ros - es and whisk - ers on kit - tens, bright cop - per
2. *See additional lyrics*

ket - tles and warm wool - en mit - tens, brown pa - per pack - ag - es

tied up with strings, these are a few of my fa - vor - ite things.

fa - vor - ite things. When the dog bites, when the

bee stings, when I'm feel - ing sad, _____ I

sim - ply re - mem - ber my fa - vor - ite things and then I don't

feel _____ so bad.

Additional Lyrics

2. Cream colored ponies and crisp apple strudels,
   Doorbells and sleighbells and schnitzel with noodles,
   Wild geese that fly with the moon on their wings,
   These are a few of my favorite things.

The Night Before Christmas Song

Music by Johnny Marks
Lyrics adapted by Johnny Marks from Clement Moore's Poem

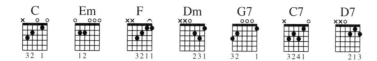

C   Em   F   Dm   G7   C7   D7

Strum Pattern: 8
Pick Pattern: 8

Verse
Brightly

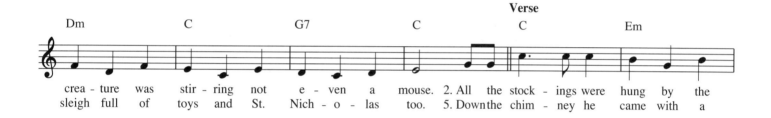

1. 'Twas the night be - fore Christ - mas and all through the house, not a
up to the house - top the rein - deer soon flew, with the

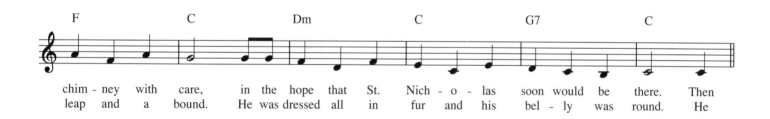

crea - ture was stir - ring not e - ven a mouse. 2. All the stock - ings were hung by the
sleigh full of toys and St. Nich - o - las too. 5. Down the chim - ney he came with a

Verse

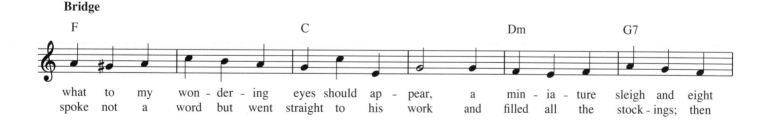

chim - ney with care, in the hope that St. Nich - o - las soon would be there. Then
leap and a bound. He was dressed all in fur and his bel - ly was round. He

Bridge

what to my won - der - ing eyes should ap - pear, a min - ia - ture sleigh and eight
spoke not a word but went straight to his work and filled all the stock - ings; then

ti - ny rein - deer. A lit - tle old driv - er so live - ly and
turned with a jerk. And lay - ing his fin - ger a - side of his

D7

quick, I knew in a mo-ment it must be St. Nick. 3. And more
nose, then giv-ing a nod up the chim-ney he rose; 6. But I

Verse

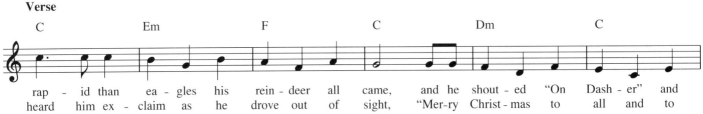

C **Em** **F** **C** **Dm** **C**

rap - id than ea - gles his rein-deer all came, and he shout-ed "On Dash - er" and
heard him ex - claim as he drove out of sight, "Mer-ry Christ-mas to all and to

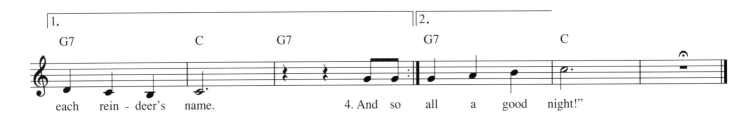

1.
G7 **C** **G7** **2.** **G7** **C**

each rein - deer's name. 4. And so all a good night!"

Nuttin' for Christmas

Words and Music by Roy Bennett and Sid Tepper

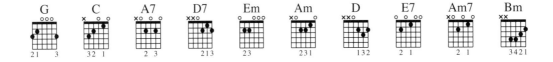

| G | C | A7 | D7 | Em | Am | D | E7 | Am7 | Bm |

Strum Pattern: 4
Pick Pattern: 5

Verse
Brightly

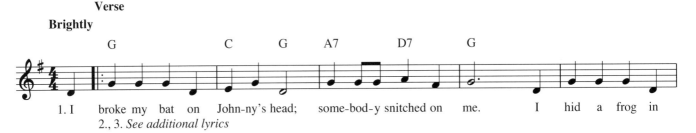

G **C** **G** **A7** **D7** **G**

1. I broke my bat on John-ny's head; some-bod-y snitched on me. I hid a frog in
2., 3. *See additional lyrics*

C **G** **A7** **D7** **G** **C** **D7**

sis-ter's bed; some-bod-y snitched on me. I spilled some ink on Mom-my's rug, I made Tom-my

G **Em** **A7** **D7** **G** **D7**

eat a bug, bought some gum with a pen - ny slug; some - bod-y snitched on me. Oh,

Chorus

I'm get - tin' nut - tin' for Christ-mas. Mom - my and Dad - dy are

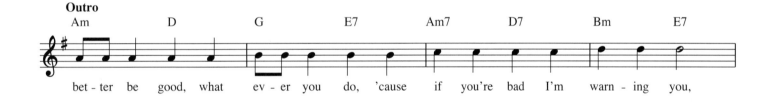

mad. I'm get - tin' nut - tin' for Christ-mas, 'cause

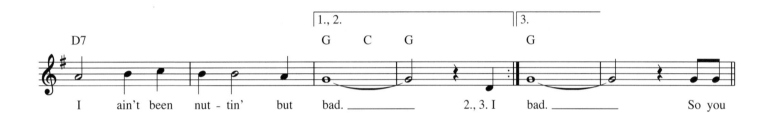

I ain't been nut - tin' but bad. _____ 2., 3. I bad. _____ So you

Outro

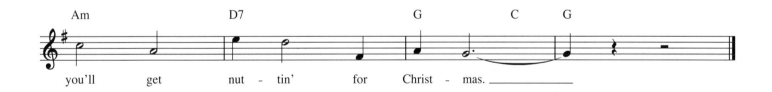

bet - ter be good, what ev - er you do, 'cause if you're bad I'm warn - ing you,

you'll get nut - tin' for Christ - mas. _____

Additional Lyrics

2. I put a tack on teacher's chair;
   Somebody snitched on me.
   I tied a knot in Susie's hair;
   Somebody snitched on me.
   I did a dance on Mommy's plants,
   Climbed a tree and tore my pants.
   Filled the sugar bowl with ants;
   Somebody snitched on me.

3. I won't be seeing Santa Claus;
   Somebody snitched on me.
   He won't come visit me because
   Somebody snitched on me.
   Next year, I'll be going straight.
   Next year, I'll be good, just wait.
   I'd start now but it's too late;
   Somebody snitched on me, oh,

Old Toy Trains

Words and Music by Roger Miller

Strum Pattern: 3
Pick Pattern: 3

Chorus
Moderately

Old toy trains, ___ lit-tle toy ___ tracks, ___ lit-tle toy ___ drums, ___

___ com-in' from a sack, car-ried by a man dressed in white and

red. Lit-tle boy ___ don't ___ you think it's time you were in bed? Close your

Bridge

eyes, _____ lis-ten to the skies. _____

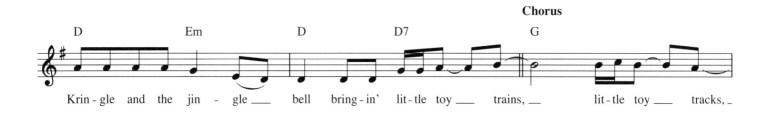

___ All is calm, all is well; soon you'll hear Kris

Chorus

Krin-gle and the jin - gle ___ bell bring-in' lit-tle toy ___ trains, ___ lit-tle toy ___ tracks, ___

lit - tle toy ___ drums ___ com - in' from a sack, car - ried by a

man dressed in white and red. Lit-tle boy ___ don't ___ you think it's time you were in

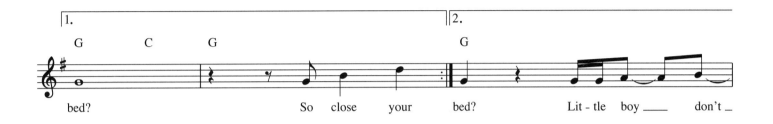

1. bed? So close your bed? **2.** Lit - tle boy ___ don't ___

___ you think it's time you were in bed?

Pretty Paper

Words and Music by Willie Nelson

Strum Pattern: 8, 7
Pick Pattern: 8, 9

G D7 G7 C A7

Verse
Slowly, with expression

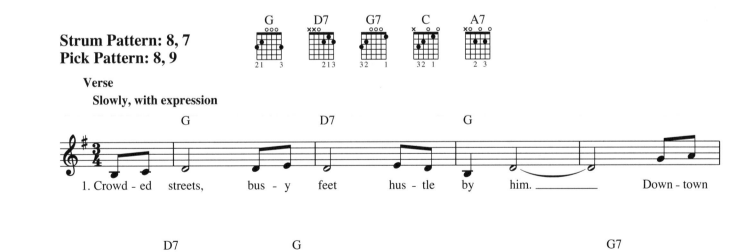

1. Crowd - ed streets, bus - y feet hus - tle by him. ___ Down - town

shop - pers, Christ - mas is nigh. ___ There he sits all a - lone on the

side - walk. _____ Hop - ing that you won't pass him by. _____ 2. Should you

Verse

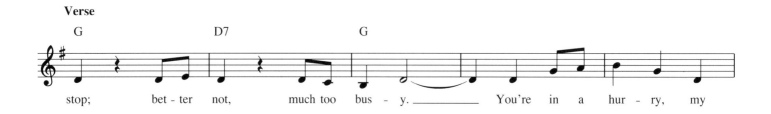

stop; bet - ter not, much too bus - y. _____ You're in a hur - ry, my

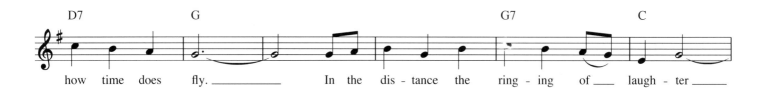

how time does fly. _____ In the dis - tance the ring - ing of ___ laugh - ter _____

___ and in the midst of the laugh - ter he cries. _____ Pret - ty

Chorus

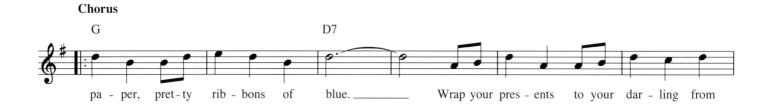

pa - per, pret - ty rib - bons of blue. _____ Wrap your pres - ents to your dar - ling from

you. _____ Pret - ty pen - cils to write, "I love you." _____ Pret - ty

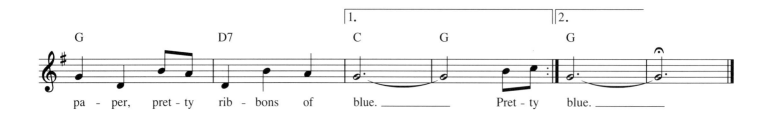

pa - per, pret - ty rib - bons of blue. _____ Pret - ty blue. _____

Rockin' Around the Christmas Tree

Music and Lyrics by Johnny Marks

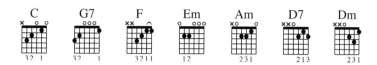

Strum Pattern: 2, 6
Pick Pattern: 4, 6

Verse
Moderate Rock

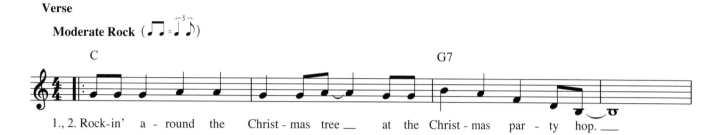

1., 2. Rock-in' a - round the Christ - mas tree ___ at the Christ - mas par - ty hop. ___

Mis - tle - toe hung where you can see ___ ev - 'ry cou - ple tries to stop.

Rock-in' a - round the Christ - mas tree, ___ let the Christ - mas spir - it ring. ___

Lat - er we'll have some pump - kin pie ___ and we'll do some car - ol - ing.

Bridge

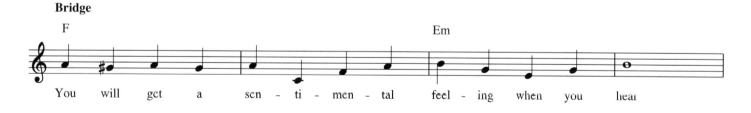

You will get a sen - ti - men - tal feel - ing when you hear

voic - es sing - ing, "Let's be jol - ly. Deck the halls with boughs of hol - ly."

Outro

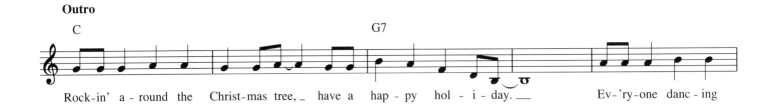

Rock-in' a - round the Christ-mas tree, _ have a hap - py hol - i - day. _ Ev-'ry-one danc - ing

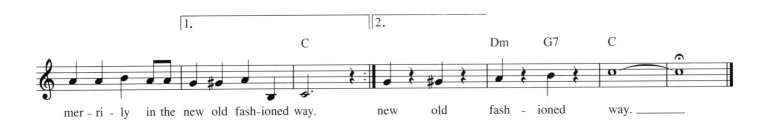

mer - ri - ly in the new old fash-ioned way. new old fash - ioned way. _____

Santa, Bring My Baby Back (To Me)

Words and Music by Claude DeMetruis and Aaron Schroeder

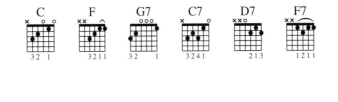

Strum Pattern: 4
Pick Pattern: 3

Verse

Moderate Rock

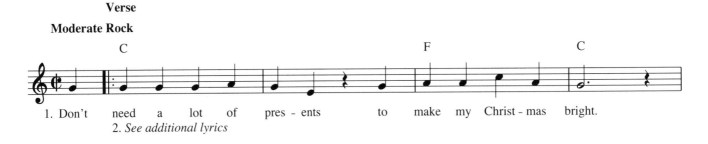

1. Don't need a lot of pres - ents to make my Christ - mas bright.
2. *See additional lyrics*

I just need my ba - by's arms wound a - round me tight. Oh, San - ta, hear my

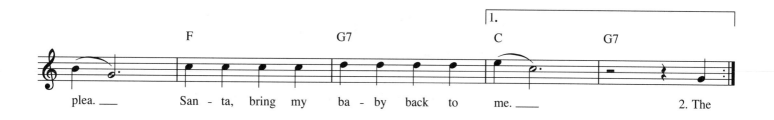

plea. ___ San - ta, bring my ba - by back to me. ___ 2. The

Bridge

me. ___ Please make those rein - deer hur - ry; the time is draw - in'

near. It sure won't seem like Christ - mas un - less my ba - by's here. Don't

Outro

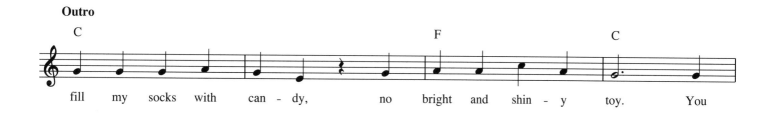

fill my socks with can - dy, no bright and shin - y toy. You

wan - na make me hap - py and fill my heart with joy. Then, San - ta, hear my

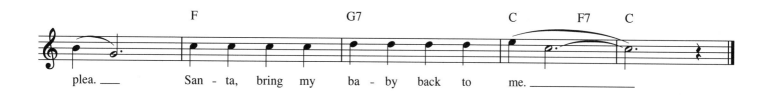

plea. ___ San - ta, bring my ba - by back to me. _____

Additional Lyrics

2. The Christmas tree is ready.
   The candles all aglow.
   But with my baby far away
   What good is mistletoe?
   Oh, Santa, hear my plea.
   Santa, bring my baby back to me.

Please Come Home for Christmas

Words and Music by Charles Brown and Gene Redd

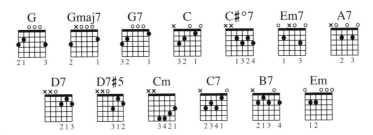

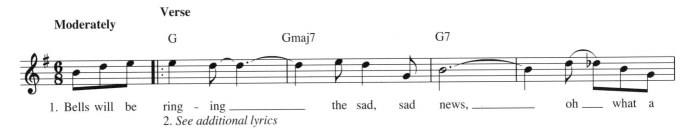

Strum Pattern: 8
Pick Pattern: 8

Moderately   **Verse**

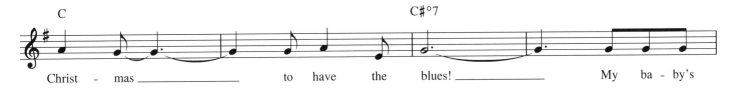

G   Gmaj7   G7

1. Bells will be ring - ing _____ the sad, sad news, _____ oh ___ what a

2. *See additional lyrics*

C   C♯°7

Christ - mas _____ to have the blues! _____ My ba - by's

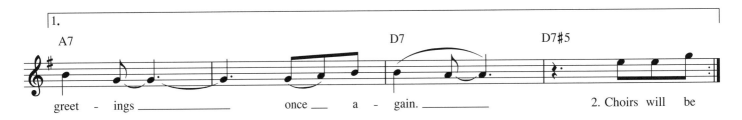

G   C   G   Em7

gone, _____ I have no friends _____ to wish me

1.

A7   D7   D7♯5

greet - ings _____ once __ a - gain. _____ 2. Choirs will be

2.

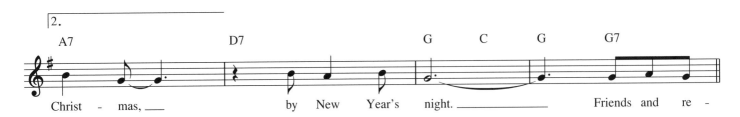

A7   D7   G   C   G   G7

Christ - mas, ___ by New Year's night. _____ Friends and re -

Bridge

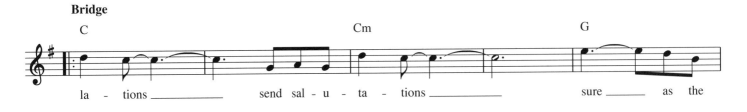

C   Cm   G

la - tions _____ send sal - u - ta - tions _____ sure ___ as the

stars   shine   a - bove. _____   For this   is   Christ - mas, _____   yes, Christ - mas   my

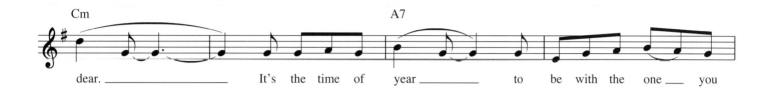

dear. _____   It's   the   time   of   year _____   to   be   with   the   one ___   you

Verse

love.   3., 4. So   won't   you   tell   me _____   you'll   nev - er - more

roam, _____   Christ - mas   and   New   Year _____   will   find   you   at

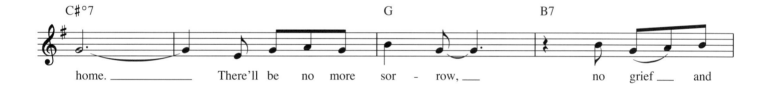

home. _____   There'll   be   no   more   sor - row, ___   no   grief ___   and

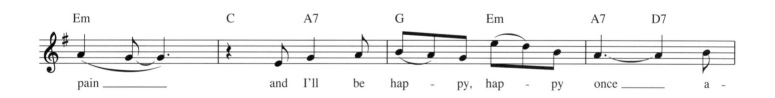

pain _____   and   I'll   be   hap - py,   hap - py   once _____   a -

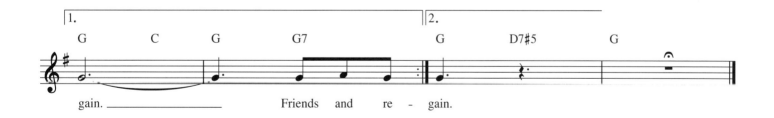

gain. _____   Friends   and   re - gain.

Additional Lyrics

2. Choirs will be singing "Silent Night,"
   Christmas carols by candlelight.
   Please come home for Christmas,
   Please come home for Christmas;
   If not for Christmas, by New Year's night.

Rudolph the Red-Nosed Reindeer

Music and Lyrics by Johnny Marks

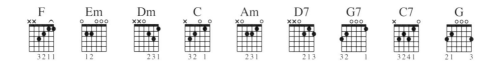

Intro
Freely

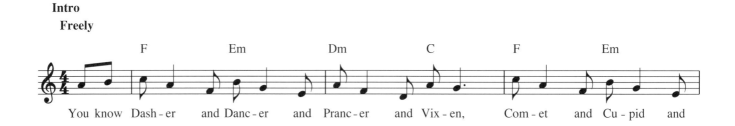

You know Dash-er and Danc-er and Pranc-er and Vix-en, Com-et and Cu-pid and

Don-ner and Blitz-en, but do you re-call the most fa-mous rein-deer of all?

Strum Pattern: 2, 3
Pick Pattern: 2, 3

Verse

Lightly

1., 2. Ru-dolph, the red-nosed rein-deer had a ver-y shin-y nose,

and if you ev-er saw it, you would e-ven say it glows.

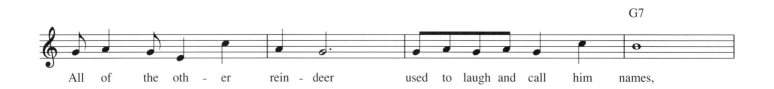

All of the oth-er rein-deer used to laugh and call him names,

they nev - er let poor Ru - dolph join in an - y rein - deer games.

Bridge

Then one fog - gy Christ - mas Eve, San - ta came to say,

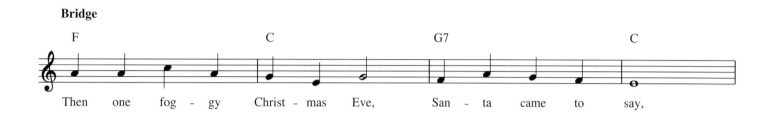

"Ru - dolph, with your nose so bright, won't you guide my sleigh to - night?" _

Outro

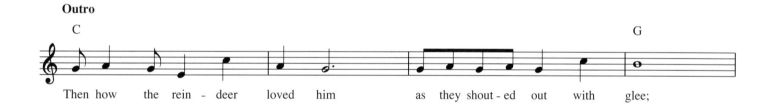

Then how the rein - deer loved him as they shout - ed out with glee;

1.

"Ru - dolph, the red - nosed rein - deer, you'll go down in his - to - ry!"

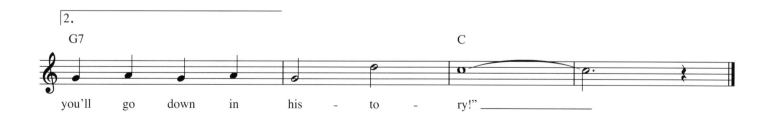

2.

you'll go down in his - to - ry!" _____

Santa Claus Is Comin' to Town

Words by Haven Gillespie
Music by J. Fred Coots

Strum Pattern: 4
Pick Pattern: 4

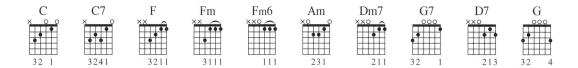

Verse

Moderately bright

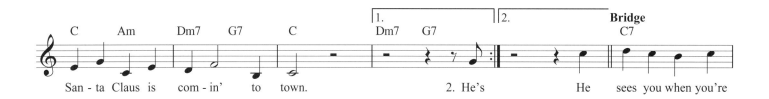

1. You bet-ter watch out, you bet-ter not cry, bet-ter not pout, I'm tell-ing you why:
   mak-ing a list and check-ing it twice, gon-na find out who's naugh-ty and nice.

San-ta Claus is com-in' to town. 2. He's He sees you when you're

sleep-in'. He knows when you're a-wake. He knows if you've been bad or good, so be

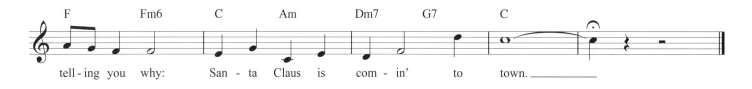

good for good-ness sake. Oh! You bet-ter watch out, you bet-ter not cry, bet-ter not pout, I'm

tell-ing you why: San-ta Claus is com-in' to town. _____

Shake Me I Rattle
(Squeeze Me I Cry)

Words and Music by Hal Hackady and Charles Naylor

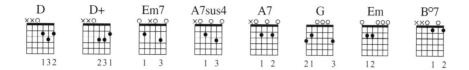

D   D+   Em7   A7sus4   A7   G   Em   B°7

Strum Pattern: 7
Pick Pattern: 7

Intro   Verse

Moderately

I was pass - ing by a toy shop on the
called an - oth - er toy shop on a
late and snow was fall - ing as the

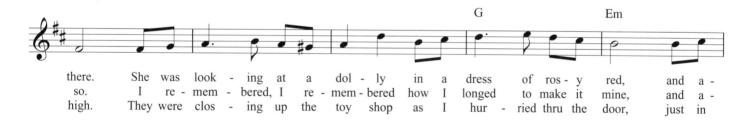

cor - ner of the square, where a lit - tle girl was look - ing in the win - dow
square so long a - go, where I saw a lit - tle dol - ly that I want - ed
shop - pers hur - ried by past the girl - ie at the win - dow with her lit - tle head held

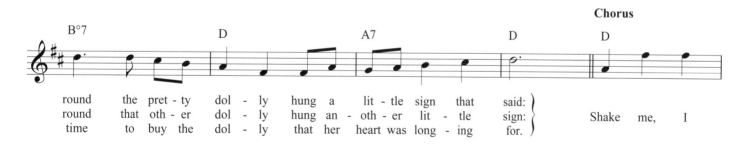

there. She was look - ing at a dol - ly in a dress of ros - y red, and a -
so. I re - mem - bered, I re - mem - bered how I longed to make it mine, and a -
high. They were clos - ing up the toy shop as I hur - ried thru the door, just in

Chorus

round the pret - ty dol - ly hung a lit - tle sign that said: Shake me, I
round that oth - er dol - ly hung an - oth - er lit - tle sign:
time to buy the dol - ly that her heart was long - ing for.

rat - tle,   squeeze me I cry.   As I stood there be - side her
                                    I had count - ed my pen - nies.
                                    And I gave her the dol - ly that we

I could hear her sigh.
Just a pen - ny shy.
both had longed to buy.
Shake me I rat - tle, squeeze me I

cry. Please take me home and love _ me. _____

1. I re -
2. It was

This Christmas

Words and Music by Donny Hathaway and Nadine McKinnor

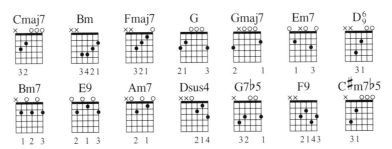

*Strum Pattern: 2
*Pick Pattern: 4

Intro
Moderately

* Use Patterns 7 & 9 for ¾ meas.

Verse

1., 4. Hang all the mis - tle - toe. _
2. Pres - ents and cards are here. _
3. *Instrumental*

I'm gon - na get to know you bet - ter, _____

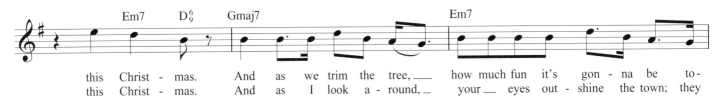

this Christ - mas. And as we trim the tree, _ how much fun it's gon - na be to-
this Christ - mas. And as I look a - round, _ your _ eyes out - shine the town; they

Silver and Gold

Music and Lyrics by Johnny Marks

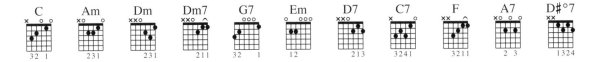

Strum Pattern: 8
Pick Pattern: 8

Verse
Slowly

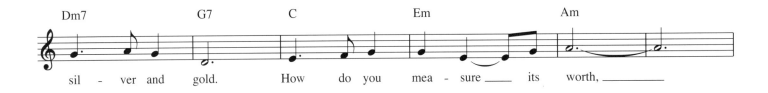

1., 2. Sil - ver and gold, sil - ver and gold, ev - 'ry - one wish - es for

sil - ver and gold. How do you mea - sure ____ its worth, ____

just by the plea - sure ____ it gives here on earth? Sil - ver and gold,

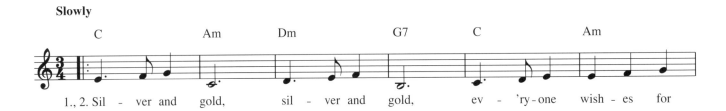

sil - ver and gold, mean so much more when I see ____ sil - ver and

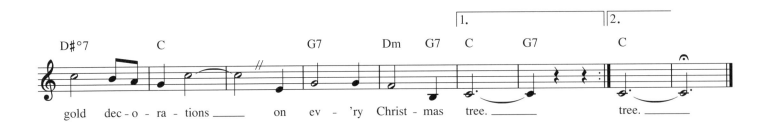

gold dec - o - ra - tions ____ on ev - 'ry Christ - mas tree. ____ tree. ____

Silver Bells

from the Paramount Picture THE LEMON DROP KID

Words and Music by Jay Livingston and Ray Evans

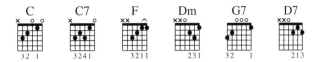

Strum Pattern: 9
Pick Pattern: 8

Verse
Moderately

1. Cit-y side-walks, bus-y side-walks dressed in hol-i-day style, in the air there's a
2. *See additional lyrics*

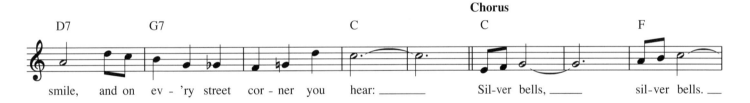

feel-ing ____ of Christ-mas. ____ Chil-dren laugh-ing, peo-ple pass-ing, meet-ing smile af-ter

Chorus

smile, and on ev-'ry street cor-ner you hear: ____ Sil-ver bells, ____ sil-ver bells. ____

____ It's Christ-mas time in the cit-y. Ring-a-ling, ____ hear them ring. ____

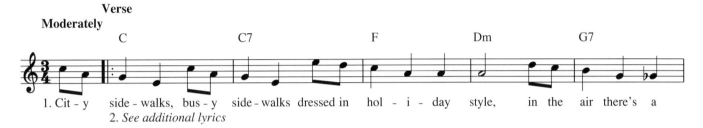

____ Soon it will be Christ-mas day. 2. Strings of day. ____

Additional Lyrics

2. Strings of street lights, even stop lights
   Blink a bright red and green,
   As the shoppers rush home with their treasures.
   Hear the snow crunch, see the kids bunch,
   This is Santa's big scene,
   And above all the bustle you hear:

Sleigh Ride

Music by Leroy Anderson
Words by Mitchell Parish

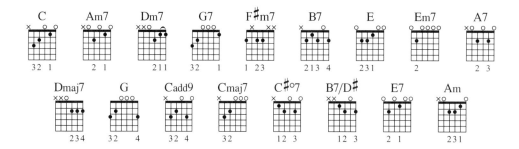

Strum Pattern: 3
Pick Pattern: 3

%‌ Verse

Moderately

N.C.

1. Just hear those (3.) sleigh bells jin - gl - ing, ring ting tin - gl - ing

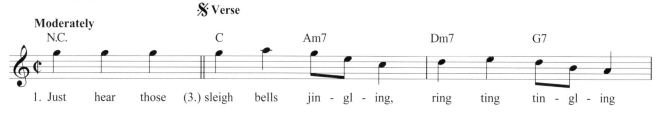

too. Come on, it's love - ly weath - er for a

sleigh ride to - geth - er with you. Out - side the

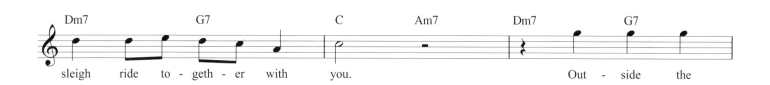

snow is fall - ing and friends are call - ing, "Yoo hoo." Come on, it's

love - ly weath - er for a sleigh ride to - geth - er with you. Gid - dy -

Bridge

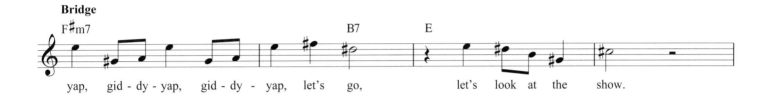

yap, gid - dy - yap, gid - dy - yap, let's go, let's look at the show.

We're rid - ing in a won - der - land of snow. Gid - dy -

yap, gid - dy - yap, gid - dy - yap, it's grand just hold - ing your hand.

We're glid - ing a - long with a song of a win - ter - y fair - y - land 2., 4. Our cheeks are

nice and ros-y and com-fy, co-zy are we. We're snug-gled

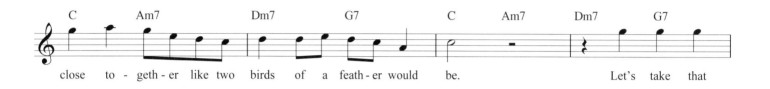

close to-geth-er like two birds of a feath-er would be. Let's take that

road be-fore us and sing a cho-rus or two. Come on, it's

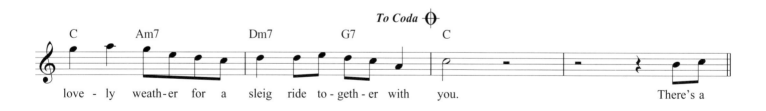

love-ly weath-er for a sleig ride to-geth-er with you. There's a

birth-day par-ty at the home of farm-er Gray. It-'ll be the per-fect
hap-py feel-ing noth-ing in the world can buy when they pass a-round the

end - ing of a per - fect day. We'll be sing - ing the songs we
cof - fee and the pump - kin pie. It - 'll near - ly be like a

love to sing with - out a sin - gle stop at the fire - place where we'll
pic - ture print by Cur - ri - er and

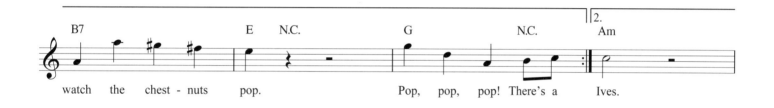

watch the chest - nuts pop. Pop, pop, pop! There's a Ives.

D.S. al Coda

These won - der - ful things are the things we re - mem-ber all through our lives. Just hear those

⊕ Coda

Repeat & fade

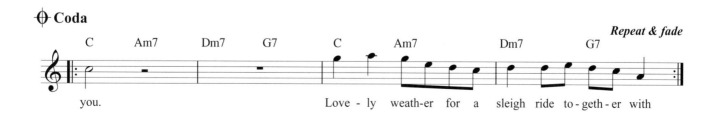

you. Love - ly weath-er for a sleigh ride to - geth - er with

Some Children See Him

Lyric by Wihla Hutson
Music by Alfred Burt

*Strum Pattern: 7 & 10
*Pick Pattern: 7 & 10

Verse

Slowly

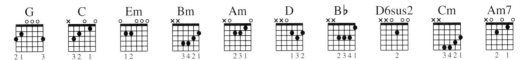

1. Some chil-dren see Him lil-y white, the Ba-by Je-sus born this night. Some
2., 3. *See additional lyrics*

*Combine Patterns for 𝄵

chil-dren see Him lil-y white, with tress-es soft and fair. Some

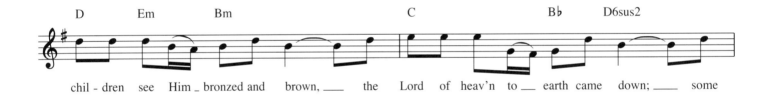

chil-dren see Him bronzed and brown, the Lord of heav'n to earth came down; some

chil-dren see Him bronzed and brown, with dark and heav-y hair. 2. Some love that's born to-night!

Additional Lyrics

2. Some children see Him almond eyed,
This Savior whom we kneel beside.
Some children see Him almond eyed,
With skin of yellow hue.
Some children see Him dark as they,
Sweet Mary's Son to whom we pray;
Some children see Him dark as they,
And ah! They love Him too!

3. The children in each diff'rent place
Will see the Baby Jesus' face
Like theirs, but bright with heav'nly grace;
And filled with holy light.
O lay aside each earthly thing,
And with thy heart as offering,
Come worship now the infant King,
'Tis love that's born tonight!

Somewhere in My Memory

from the Twentieth Century Fox Motion Picture HOME ALONE

Words by Leslie Bricusse
Music by John Williams

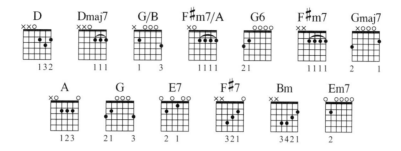

Strum Pattern: 3
Pick Pattern: 3

Verse
Moderately slow

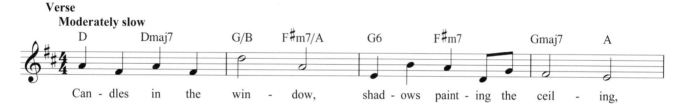

Can - dles in the win - dow, shad - ows paint - ing the ceil - ing,

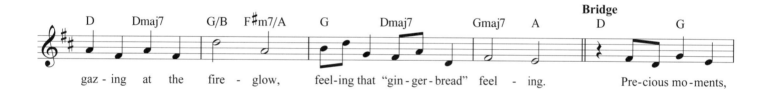

gaz - ing at the fire - glow, feel - ing that "gin - ger - bread" feel - ing. Pre - cious mo - ments,

spe - cial peo - ple, hap - py fac - es I can see. Some - where in my mem - 'ry,

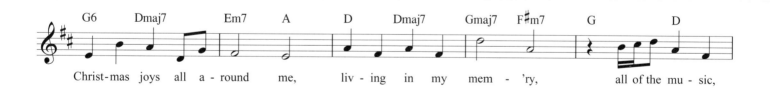

Christ - mas joys all a - round me, liv - ing in my mem - 'ry, all of the mu - sic,

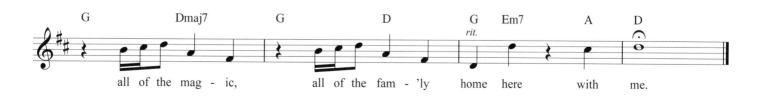

all of the mag - ic, all of the fam - 'ly home here with me.

Someday at Christmas

Words and Music by Ronald N. Miller and Bryan Wells

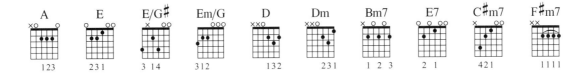

Strum Pattern: 3, 4
Pick Pattern: 3, 6

Intro
Moderately

Verse

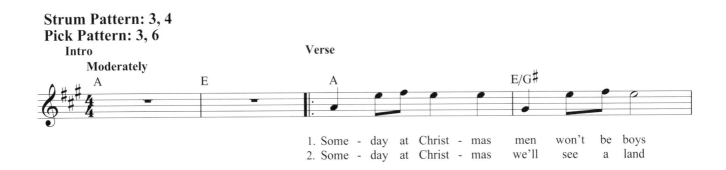

1. Some - day at Christ - mas men won't be boys
2. Some - day at Christ - mas we'll see a land

play - ing with bombs like kids play with toys. One warm De - cem - ber
with no hun - gry chil - dren, no emp - ty hand. One hap - py morn - ing

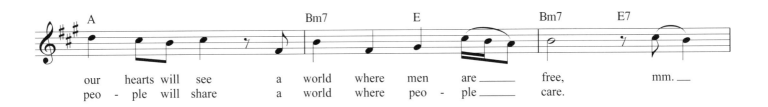

our hearts will see a world where men are _____ free, mm. _____
peo - ple will share a world where peo - ple _____ care.

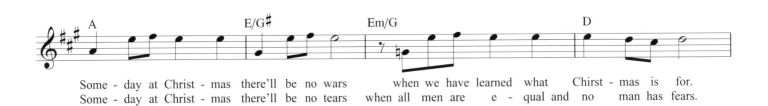

Some - day at Christ - mas there'll be no wars when we have learned what Chirst - mas is for.
Some - day at Christ - mas there'll be no tears when all men are e - qual and no man has fears.

When we have found what life's real - ly worth there'll be peace on _____ earth.
One shin - ing mo - ment, one prayer a - way from our world to - day.

Chorus

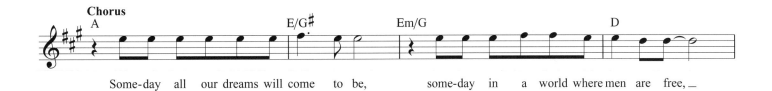

Some-day all our dreams will come to be, some-day in a world where men are free, _

may - be not in time for you and me, _ but some - day at Christ - mas time.

Verse

3. Some - day at Christ - mas man will not fail; hate will be gone and love _ will pre - vail.

Some - day a new world that we can start _ with hope in ev - 'ry heart. _

Outro-Chorus

Some - day all our dreams will come to be, some - day in a world where

men are free, may - be not in time for you and me, _ but

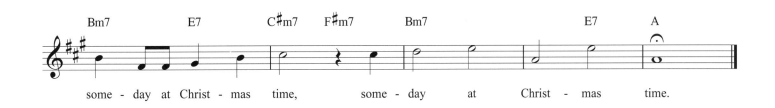

some - day at Christ - mas time, some - day at Christ - mas time.

The Star Carol

Lyric by Wihla Hutson

Music by Alfred Burt

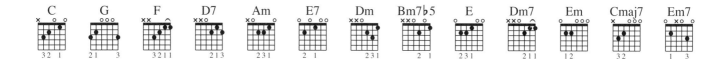

Strum Pattern: 8
Pick Pattern: 8

Verse
Tenderly

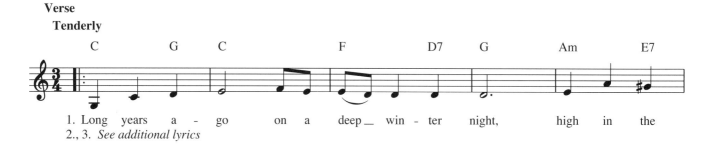

1. Long years a - go on a deep — win - ter night, high in the
2., 3. *See additional lyrics*

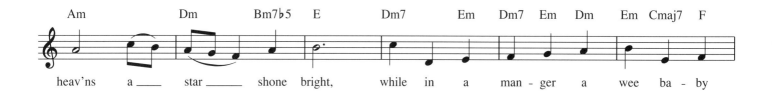

heav'ns a — star — shone bright, while in a man - ger a wee ba - by

lay. Sweet - ly a - sleep on a bed of hay. Thee.

Additional Lyrics

2. Jesus, the Lord was that Baby so small,
Laid down to sleep in a humble stall;
Then came the star and it stood overhead,
Shedding its light 'round His little bed.

3. Dear Baby Jesus, how tiny Thou art,
I'll make a place for Thee in my heart,
And when the stars in the heavens I see,
Ever and always I'll think of Thee.

Suzy Snowflake

Words and Music by Sid Tepper and Roy Bennett

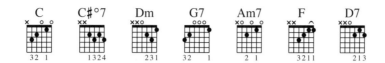

Strum Pattern: 3
Pick Pattern: 3

Verse
Moderately

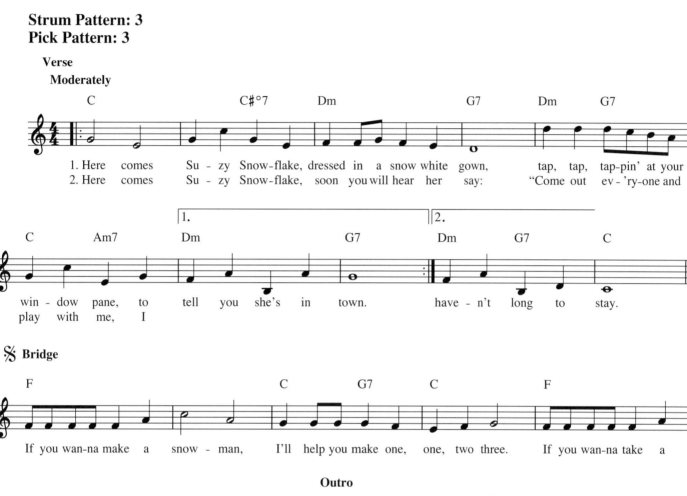

1. Here comes Su-zy Snow-flake, dressed in a snow white gown, tap, tap, tap-pin' at your
2. Here comes Su-zy Snow-flake, soon you will hear her say: "Come out ev-'ry-one and

win-dow pane, to tell you she's in town. have-n't long to stay.
play with me, I

%S Bridge

If you wan-na make a snow-man, I'll help you make one, one, two three. If you wan-na take a

Outro

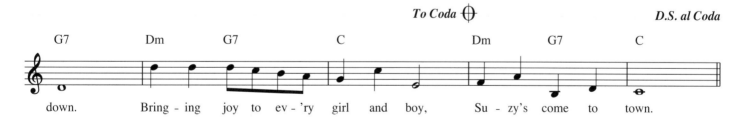

sleigh ride, the ride's on me." Here comes Su-zy Snow-flake, look at her tum-blin'

To Coda ⊕   *D.S. al Coda*

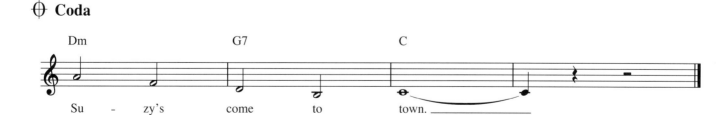

down. Bring-ing joy to ev-'ry girl and boy, Su-zy's come to town.

⊕ Coda

Su - zy's come to town. _____

This Is Christmas
(Bright, Bright the Holly Berries)

Lyric by Wihla Hutson
Music by Alfred Burt

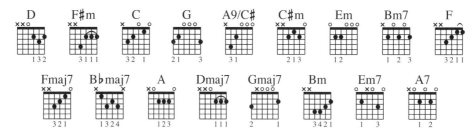

Strum Pattern: 7, 9

Pick Pattern: 7, 8

Verse

Liltingly

1. Bright bright the hol - ly ber - ries in the wreath up - on the door.
2., 3. *See additional lyrics*

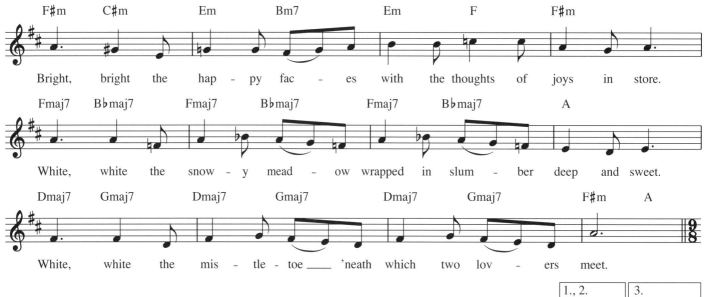

Bright, bright the hap - py fac - es with the thoughts of joys in store.

White, white the snow - y mead - ow wrapped in slum - ber deep and sweet.

White, white the mis - tle - toe ___ 'neath which two lov - ers meet.

Chorus

This is Christ - mas, this is Christ - mas, this is Christ - mas time. ___

Additional Lyrics

2. Gay, gay the children's voices filled with laughter, filled with glee.
Gay, gay the tinsled things upon the dark and spicy tree.
Day, day when all mankind may hear the angel's song again.
Day, day when Christ was born to bless the sons of men.

3. Sing, sing ye heav'nly host to tell the blessed Saviour's birth.
Sing, sing in holy joy, ye dwellers all upon the earth.
King, King yet tiny Babe, come down to us from God above.
King, King of ev'ry heart which opens wide to love.

What Are You Doing New Year's Eve?

By Frank Loesser

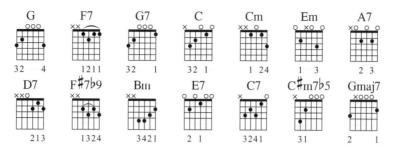

Strum Pattern: 5
Pick Pattern: 5

Verse
Moderately

1., 4. May-be it's much too ear-ly in the game, __ ah, but I thought I'd

ask you just the same, __ what are you do-ing New Year's, New Year's

Eve? 2., 5. Won-der whose arms will hold you good and tight, __

when it's ex-act-ly twelve o'-clock that night, __ wel-com-ing in the

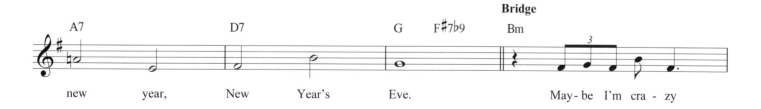

new year, New Year's Eve. May-be I'm cra-zy

to sup-pose I'd ev-er be the one you chose

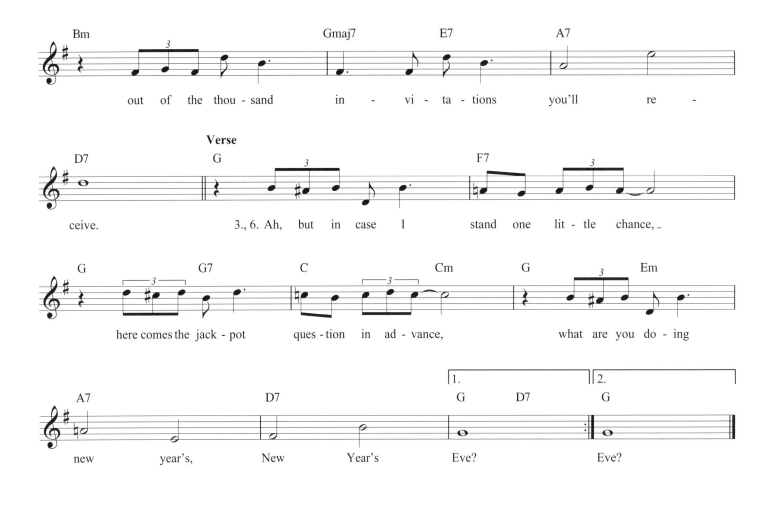

out of the thou - sand in - vi - ta - tions you'll re -

Verse

ceive. 3., 6. Ah, but in case I stand one lit - tle chance,

here comes the jack - pot ques - tion in ad - vance, what are you do - ing

1.   2.

new year's, New Year's Eve? Eve?

The White World of Winter

Words by Mitchell Parish
Music by Hoagy Carmichael

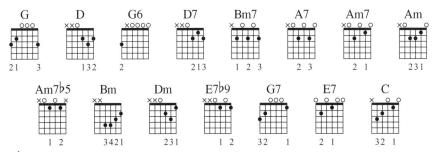

Strum Pattern: 4
Pick Pattern: 3

Verse

Moderately

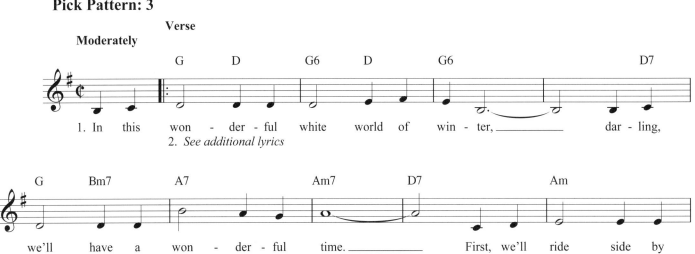

1. In this won - der - ful white world of win - ter, _____ dar - ling,
2. *See additional lyrics*

we'll have a won - der - ful time. _____ First, we'll ride side by

Additional Lyrics

2. In this wonderful white world of winter,
   Darling, we'll have a wonderful time;
   If we prayed it would snow all this winter
   I as ya, is that a terr'ble, horr'ble crime?
   I can't wait till we skate on Lake Happy
   And sup a hot buttered cup in the afterglow.
   If there's ever a moment you're not laughin',
   Maybe a toboggan; split your little noggin'.
   In this wonderful white world of winter,
   I'm thinkin' you are the sweetest one I know.

We Need a Little Christmas

from MAME

Music and Lyric by Jerry Herman

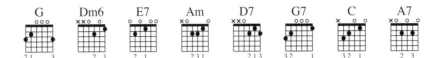

Strum Pattern: 4
Pick Pattern: 1

Verse

Brightly

G

1. Haul out the hol - ly. _____ Put up the
climb down the chim - ney, _____ turn on the

Dm6   E7

tree be - fore my spir - it falls _____ a - gain.
bright - est string of lights I've ev - er seen.

Am   D7   Am   D7

Fill up the stock - ing. _____ I may be
Slice up the fruit - cake. _____ It's time we

Am   D7

rush - ing things, but deck the halls _____ a - gain
hung some tin - sel on the ev - er - green

Dm6   E7   Am   E7

now. _____
bough. _____
                                For we
                                For I've
                                For we

Am   D7   G

need a lit - tle Christ - mas, right this ver - y min - ute,
grown a lit - tle lean - er, grown a lit - tle cold - er,
need a lit - tle mu - sic, need a lit - tle laugh - ter,

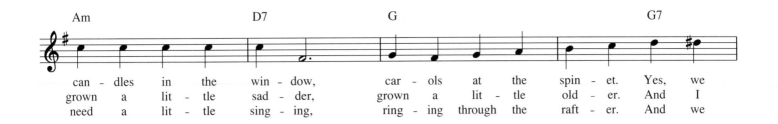

can - dles in the win - dow, car - ols at the spin - et. Yes, we
grown a lit - tle sad - der, grown a lit - tle old - er. And I
need a lit - tle sing - ing, ring - ing through the raft - er. And we

To Coda ⊕

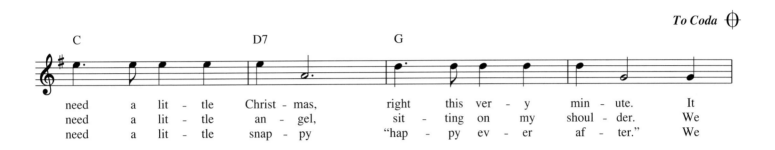

need a lit - tle Christ - mas, right this ver - y min - ute. It
need a lit - tle an - gel, sit - ting on my shoul - der. We
need a lit - tle snap - py "hap - py ev - er af - ter." We

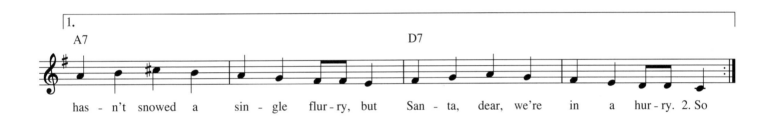

has - n't snowed a sin - gle flur - ry, but San - ta, dear, we're in a hur - ry. 2. So

D.S. al Coda

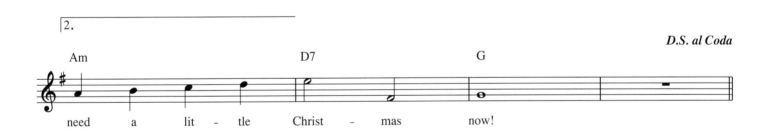

need a lit - tle Christ - mas now!

⊕ **Coda**

need a lit - tle Christ - mas now! _____

What a Merry Christmas This Could Be

Words and Music by Hank Cochran and Harlan Howard

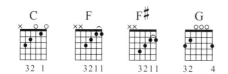

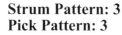

Strum Pattern: 3
Pick Pattern: 3

Chorus
Moderate Country

What a mer - ry Christ - mas this could be if you __

__ would just come back __ to __ me ____ and

say that you'd for - giv - en __ me. ____ What a mer -

- ry Christ - mas this __ could __ be. _____

Verse

It was just __ last Christ - mas that we quar - reled and you walked out. __ I knew __

__ I was wrong, __ but you'd __ come back; I __ had no doubt. Now a year __

____ has rolled a - round, _ it's Christ-mas once a - gain, and_

_what I'd give if you'd _ come _ walk - in' _ in. What a mer -_

Chorus

_- ry Christ - mas this could be if you __

2nd time, Instrumental

___ would just come back ___ to ___ me _____ and_

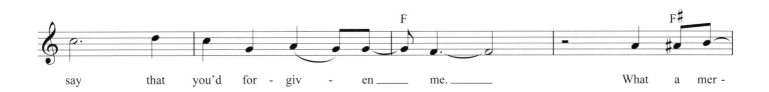

_say that you'd for - giv - en ____ me. _____ What a mer -_

_- ry Christ - mas this _ could _ be. ____ Instrumental begins What a mer -_

_What a mer - ry Christ - mas this _ could _ be. ____

What Christmas Means to Me

Words and Music by George Gordy, Allen Story and Anna Gordy Gaye

Strum Pattern: 2
Pick Pattern: 4

Intro
Brightly

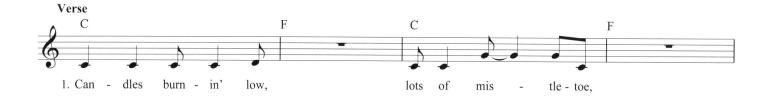

Verse

1. Can - dles burn - in' low,   lots of mis - tle - toe,

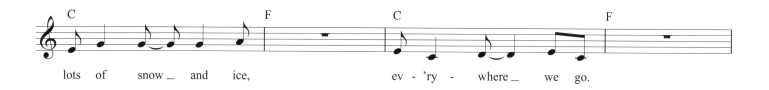

lots of snow __ and ice,   ev - 'ry - where __ we go.

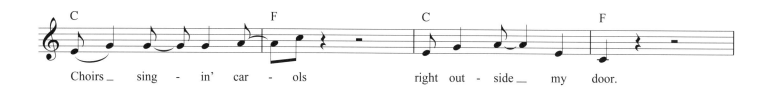

Choirs __ sing - in' car - ols   right out - side __ my door.

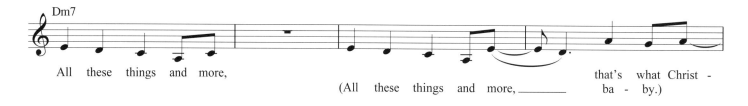

All these things and more,   (All these things and more, _____ that's what Christ - ba - by.)

- mas means __ to me, __ my love. (That's what Christ - mas means to me, __ my love.) __

Interlude

2. I ____

Verse

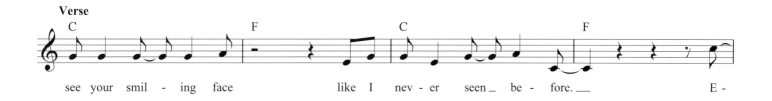

see your smil - ing face like I nev - er seen __ be - fore. __ E -

- ven though __ I love __ you mad - ly, it seems I love you more. The lit -

- tle cards __ you'll give __ me will touch __ my heart __ for sure. All __

____ these things __ and more, __ dar - lin', that's what Christ -
(All these things and more, _____ dar - lin'.)

- mas means __ to me, __ my love. (That's what Christ - mas means to me, __ my love.) __

Bridge

I feel __ like run - nin' wild, __ as anx - ious as a lit - tle child to greet __

__ you 'neath __ the mis - tle - toe, kiss you once __ and then __ some more. And

157

wish you a mer - ry Christ - mas, ba - by,
(Wish you a mer - ry Christ - mas, ba - by.)
and such

hap - pi - ness in the com - ing year. __ Whoa, ba - by. 3. Let's deck __

Verse

__ the halls __ with hol - ly, sing sweet "Si - lent Night,"

fill a tree __ with an - gel hair __ and pret - ty, pret - ty lights, __

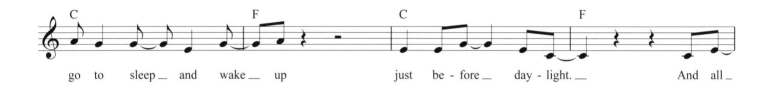

go to sleep __ and wake __ up just be - fore __ day - light. __ And all __

__ these things and more, __ ba - by,
(All these things and more, __ ba - by.)
that's __ what Christ -

- mas means __ to me, __ my love. (That's what Christ - mas means to me, __ my love.) __

Outro

Repeat and fade

158

Where Are You Christmas?

from DR. SEUSS' HOW THE GRINCH STOLE CHRISTMAS

Words and Music by Will Jennings, James Horner and Mariah Carey

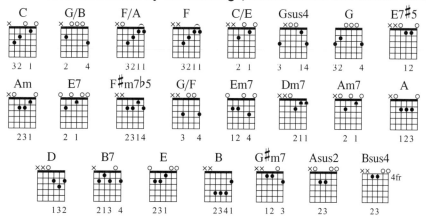

Strum Pattern: 2
Pick Pattern: 2, 4

Intro
Gently

1. Where are you,

Christ - mas? Why can't I find you? Why have you

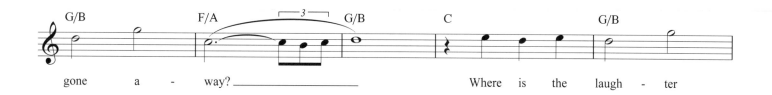

gone a - way? _____ Where is the laugh - ter

you used to bring me? Why can't I hear mu - sic play? _____

My world is chang - ing. ___ I'm re - ar -

rang - ing. Does that mean Christ - mas chang -

- es too? ___

Verse

2. Where are you, Christ - mas? Do you re - mem - ber the one you

used to know? ___ I'm not the

same one. __ See what the time's done. Is that why you ___ have

let ___ me go? ___ Oh, ___

Bridge

Christ - mas is here, ___ ev - 'ry - where, ___ oh.

Christ - mas is here, __ if you care. __

If there is love __ in your heart and __ your mind, __

you will feel like Christ - mas all the time. __ Oh, I feel you,

Outro-Verse

Christ - mas, __ I know I found you. You nev - er fade a -

way. __ Oh, the joy of Christ - mas __ stays here in -

side us, fills each and ev - 'ry heart __ with love. __

A tempo

Where are you Christ - mas?

Fill your heart with love. Mm. __

White Christmas

from the Motion Picture Irving Berlin's HOLIDAY INN

Words and Music by Irving Berlin

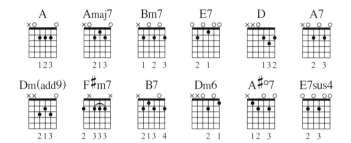

Strum Pattern: 3
Pick Pattern: 3

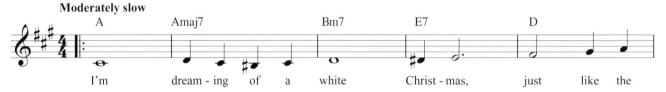

I'm dream-ing of a white Christ-mas, just like the

ones I used to know. Where the tree tops glis-ten and

chil-dren lis-ten to hear sleigh bells in the snow. _____

I'm dream-ing of a white Christ-mas with ev-'ry Christ-mas card I

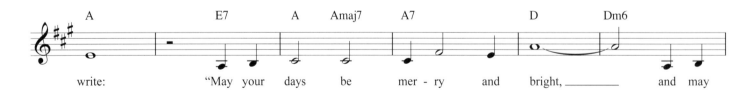

write: "May your days be mer-ry and bright, _____ and may

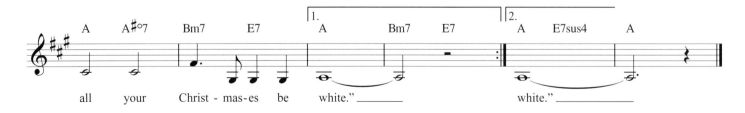

all your Christ-mas-es be white." _____ white." _____

Why Christmas

Words and Music by Wanya Morris

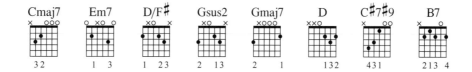

Strum Pattern: 6
Pick Pattern: 4

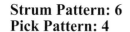

look - in' for Mom _ but she's _ not there. _ Kids are look - ing for rein - deer in _

D/F#   Gsus2   Gmaj7

_ the air. _____ She messed up a - gain. _____ Why? _

𝄋 Chorus

Cmaj7   D

_ My _ broth - er and _ my sis - ter, they ain't got _ no toys. _

Em7

_ What am I _ sup - posed _ to do _ when grow - ing up for me was - n't joy? _

Cmaj7   D

_ It's gon - na be a why _____ Christ - mas. _ It's gon - na be, _ it's gon-

To Coda ⊕

C#7#9

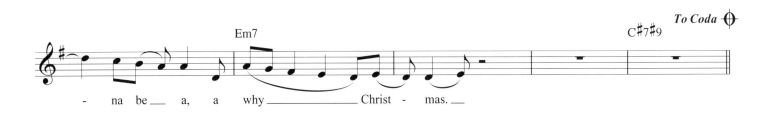

Em7

- na be a, a why _____ Christ - mas. _

Verse

Cmaj7

2. No one was there _ but Grand - ma and her _ friends; the time of heart - ache _

Em7

set - ting _ in. There ain't noth - ing _ I _____ can do _ just

164

sit ___ and feel ___ pain run ___ me through. ___ I _____ of - ten wished ___

___ they were nev - er born. ___ The thought of them hav - ing no toys and ___ their hearts were

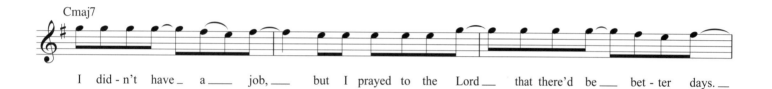

torn. ___ I was young ___ and I cried _____ as well, _____ oh, ___ yeah.

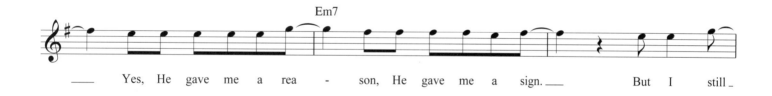

I did - n't have ___ a ___ job, ___ but I prayed to the Lord ___ that there'd be ___ bet - ter days. ___

___ Yes, He gave me a rea - son, He gave me a sign. ___ But I still _

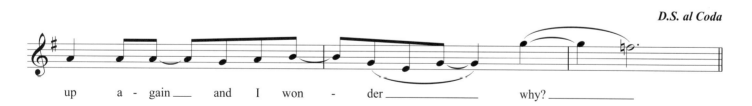

___ think to ___ that ___ day ___ when she messed up a - gain, ___ she messed

D.S. al Coda

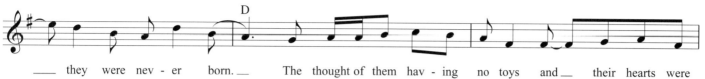

up a - gain ___ and I won - der _____ why? _____

𝄌 Coda

Repeat and fade

Bro - ther and ___ my, bro - ther and ___ my, bro - ther and ___ my sis - ter.

Wonderful Christmastime

Words and Music by Paul McCartney

Strum Pattern: 2
Pick Pattern: 4

Verse

Brightly

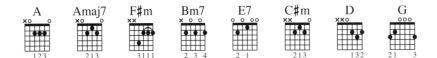

1. The mood is right, __ the spir-it's up, __
2., 3. *See additional lyrics*

we're here to - night __ and that's e - nough. __

Chorus

Sim - ply hav - ing a won - der - ful Christ - mas - time.

Sim - ply hav - ing a won - der - ful Christ - mas - time. time.

Bridge

The choir of chil - dren sing their song. (They prac - tised

To Coda

all year long.) Ding dong, ding dong. Ding dong, ding.

We're sim - ply hav - ing a won - der - ful Christ mas -

D.C. al Coda
(take 2nd ending)

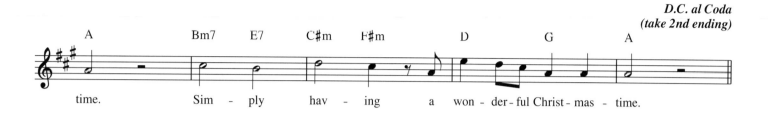

time. Sim - ply hav - ing a won - der - ful Christ - mas - time.

⊕ Coda

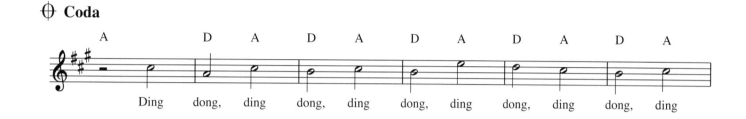

Ding dong, ding dong, ding dong, ding dong, ding dong, ding

dong, dong dong, dong, dong. The par - ty's on, ___ the spir-it's up, _

_ we're here to - night _ and that's e - nough. _

Outro

Repeat and fade

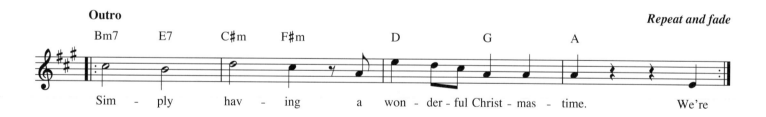

Sim - ply hav - ing a won - der - ful Christ - mas - time. We're

Additional Lyrics

2. The party's on,
   The feeling's here
   That only comes
   This time of year.

3. The word is out
   About the town,
   To lift a glass.
   Oh, don't look down.

You Make It Feel Like Christmas

Words and Music by Neil Diamond

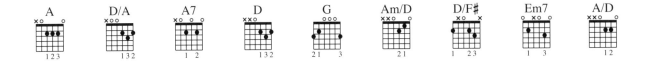

Strum Pattern: 4
Pick Pattern: 3

Intro

Moderately slow Rock

Co - zy we are, clos - er than far, sounds of for - ev - er still _

Verse

_ a - round. 1. Lov - ers in love, just like we were 'cause
2., 3. *See additional lyrics*

be - in' a - part's a lone - ly sound. And when peo - ple ask how _

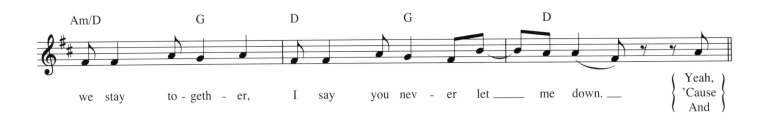

we stay to - geth - er, I say you nev - er let _ me down. _
{ Yeah, }
{ 'Cause }
{ And }

Chorus

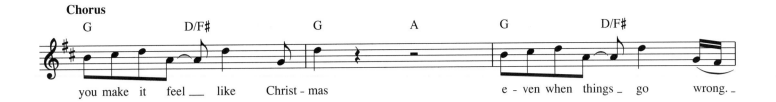

you make it feel ___ like Christ - mas   e - ven when things _ go   wrong. _

___   I hear the sound _ of   Christ - mas   in your song _

___   all   year   long.

1.   2.

That's how you know that it's true, ba - by.

3.

3. Just   Yes, you know I do babe,

all   year   long. _____

Additional Lyrics

2. Look at the sun shining on me;
Nowhere could be a better place.
Lovers in love, yeah, that's what we'll be.
When you're here with me, it's Christmas Day.

3. Just look at us now, part of it all.
In spite of it all, we're still around.
So wake up the kids, and put on some tea.
Let's light up the tree; it's Christmas Day.

Winter Wonderland

Words by Dick Smith
Music by Felix Bernard

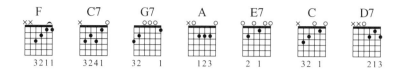

Strum Pattern: 3, 4
Pick Pattern: 3, 4

Verse

Moderately

1. Sleigh bells (4.) ring, are you lis - t'nin'? In the lane, snow is glis - t'nin'. A

beau - ti - ful sight, _ we're hap - py to - night, _ walk - in' in a win - ter won - der - land. 2., 5. Gone a -

Verse

way is the blue - bird, here to stay is a new bird;
He sings a love song, _ as
He's sing - ing a song, _ as

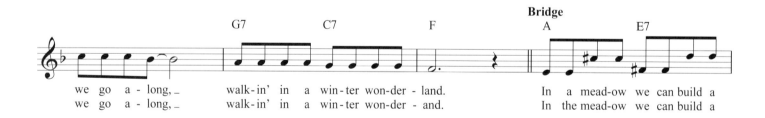

we go a - long, _ walk - in' in a win - ter won - der - land.
we go a - long, _ walk - in' in a win - ter won - der - and.
Bridge
In a mead - ow we can build a
In the mead - ow we can build a

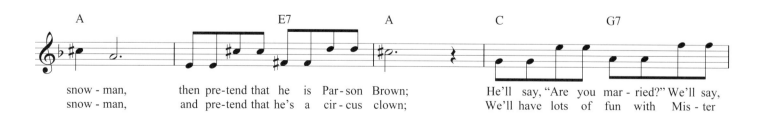

snow - man, then pre - tend that he is Par - son Brown;
snow - man, and pre - tend that he's a cir - cus clown;
He'll say, "Are you mar - ried?" We'll say,
We'll have lots of fun with Mis - ter

"No, man! But you can do the job when you're in town!" 3. Lat - er on, we'll con -
Snow - man, un - til the oth - er kid - dies knock 'im down! 6. When it snows, ain't it

spire, ___ as we dream by the fire, ___ to face un - a - fraid, _ the
thrill - in', tho' your nose gets a chill - in'? We'll frol - ic and play _ the

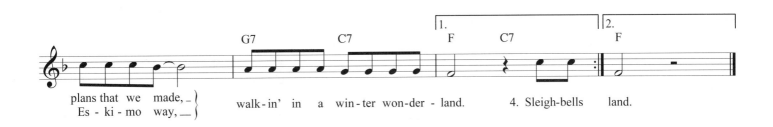

plans that we made, _ walk - in' in a win - ter won - der - land. 4. Sleigh - bells land.
Es - ki - mo way, _

STRUM & SING

Lyrics, chord symbols, and guitar chord diagrams for your favorite songs.

GUITAR

ADELE
00159855..........................$12.99

SARA BAREILLES
00102354..........................$12.99

BLUES
00159335..........................$12.99

ZAC BROWN BAND
02501620..........................$12.99

COLBIE CAILLAT
02501725..........................$14.99

CAMPFIRE FOLK SONGS
02500686..........................$12.99

CHART HITS OF 2014-2015
00142554..........................$12.99

CHART HITS OF 2015-2016
00156248..........................$12.99

BEST OF KENNY CHESNEY
00142457..........................$14.99

KELLY CLARKSON
00146384..........................$14.99

JOHN DENVER COLLECTION
02500632..........................$9.95

EAGLES
00157994..........................$12.99

EASY ACOUSTIC SONGS
00125478..........................$14.99

50 CHILDREN'S SONGS
02500825..........................$8.99

THE 5 CHORD SONGBOOK
02501718..........................$12.99

FOLK SONGS
02501482..........................$10.99

FOLK/ROCK FAVORITES
02501669..........................$10.99

THE 4 CHORD SONGBOOK
02501533..........................$12.99

THE 4-CHORD COUNTRY SONGBOOK
00114936..........................$12.99

HAMILTON
00217116..........................$14.99

HITS OF THE '60S
02501138..........................$12.99

HITS OF THE '70S
02500871..........................$9.99

HYMNS
02501125..........................$8.99

JACK JOHNSON
02500858..........................$16.99

ROBERT JOHNSON
00191890..........................$12.99

CAROLE KING
00115243..........................$10.99

BEST OF GORDON LIGHTFOOT
00139393..........................$14.99

DAVE MATTHEWS BAND
02501078..........................$10.95

JOHN MAYER
02501636..........................$10.99

INGRID MICHAELSON
02501634..........................$10.99

THE MOST REQUESTED SONGS
02501748..........................$12.99

JASON MRAZ
02501452..........................$14.99

PRAISE & WORSHIP
00152381..........................$12.99

ROCK AROUND THE CLOCK
00103625..........................$12.99

ROCK BALLADS
02500872..........................$9.95

ED SHEERAN
00152016..........................$12.99

THE 6 CHORD SONGBOOK
02502277..........................$10.99

CAT STEVENS
00116827..........................$12.99

TAYLOR SWIFT
00159856..........................$12.99

TODAY'S HITS
00119301..........................$12.99

TOP CHRISTIAN HITS
00156331..........................$12.99

KEITH URBAN
00118558..........................$14.99

NEIL YOUNG – GREATEST HITS
00138270..........................$12.99

UKULELE

COLBIE CAILLAT
02501731..........................$10.99

JOHN DENVER
02501694..........................$10.99

THE 4-CHORD UKULELE SONGBOOK
00114331..........................$14.99

JACK JOHNSON
02501702..........................$17.99

JOHN MAYER
02501706..........................$10.99

INGRID MICHAELSON
02501741..........................$12.99

THE MOST REQUESTED SONGS
02501453..........................$14.99

JASON MRAZ
02501753..........................$14.99

SING-ALONG SONGS
02501710..........................$15.99

Prices, content, and availability subject to change without notice.

www.halleonard.com
Visit our website to see full song lists.

0717

Celebrate Christmas
WITH YOUR GUITAR AND HAL LEONARD

THE BEST CHRISTMAS GUITAR FAKE BOOK EVER – 2ND EDITION

INCLUDES TAB

Over 150 Christmas classics for guitar. Songs include: Blue Christmas • The Chipmunk Song • Frosty the Snow Man • Happy Holiday • A Holly Jolly Christmas • I Saw Mommy Kissing Santa Claus • I Wonder As I Wander • Jingle-Bell Rock • Rudolph, the Red-Nosed Reindeer • Santa Bring My Baby Back (To Me) • Suzy Snowflake • Tennessee Christmas • and more.

00240053 Melody/Lyrics/Chords.............. $22.50

THE BIG CHRISTMAS COLLECTION FOR EASY GUITAR

Includes over 70 Christmas favorites, such as: Ave Maria • Blue Christmas • Deck the Hall • Feliz Navidad • Frosty the Snow Man • Happy Holiday • A Holly Jolly Christmas • Joy to the World • O Holy Night • Silver and Gold • Suzy Snowflake • and more. Does not include TAB.

00698978 Easy Guitar.............................. $16.95

CHRISTMAS

INCLUDES TAB

Guitar Play-Along Volume 22
Book/Online Audio

8 songs: The Christmas Song (Chestnuts Roasting on an Open Fire) • Frosty the Snow Man • Happy Xmas (War Is Over) • Here Comes Santa Claus (Right Down Santa Claus Lane) • Jingle-Bell Rock • Merry Christmas, Darling • Rudolph the Red-Nosed Reindeer • Silver Bells.

00699600 Guitar Tab............................... $15.99

CHRISTMAS CAROLS

Guitar Chord Songbook

80 favorite carols for guitarists who just need the lyrics and chords: Angels We Have Heard on High • Away in a Manger • Deck the Hall • Good King Wenceslas • The Holly and the Ivy • Irish Carol • Jingle Bells • Joy to the World • O Holy Night • Rocking • Silent Night • Up on the Housetop • Welsh Carol • What Child Is This? • and more.

00699536 Lyrics/Chord Symbols/
            Guitar Chord Diagrams............ $12.99

CHRISTMAS CAROLS

INCLUDES TAB

Guitar Play-Along Volume 62
Book/CD Pack

8 songs: God Rest Ye Merry, Gentlemen • Hark! The Herald Angels Sing • It Came upon the Midnight Clear • O Come, All Ye Faithful (Adeste Fideles) • O Holy Night • Silent Night • We Three Kings of Orient Are • What Child Is This?

00699798 Guitar Tab............................... $12.95

CHRISTMAS CAROLS

INCLUDES TAB

Jazz Guitar Chord Melody Solos

Chord melody arrangements in notes & tab of 26 songs of the season. Includes: Auld Lang Syne • Deck the Hall • Good King Wenceslas • Here We Come A-Wassailing • Joy to the World • O Little Town of Bethlehem • Toyland • We Three Kings of Orient Are • and more.

00701697 Solo Guitar............................... $12.99

THE CHRISTMAS GUITAR COLLECTION

INCLUDES TAB

Book/CD Pack

20 beautiful fingerstyle arrangements of contemporary Christmas favorites, including: Blue Christmas • Feliz Navidad • Happy Xmas (War Is Over) • I Saw Mommy Kissing Santa Claus • I'll Be Home for Christmas • A Marshmallow World • The Most Wonderful Time of the Year • What Are You Doing New Year's Eve? • and more. CD includes full demos of each piece.

00700181 Fingerstyle Guitar..................... $17.95

CLASSICAL GUITAR CHRISTMAS COLLECTION

INCLUDES TAB

Includes classical guitar arrangements in standard notation and tablature for more than two dozen beloved carols: Angels We Have Heard on High • Auld Lang Syne • Ave Maria • Away in a Manger • Canon in D • The First Noel • I Saw Three Ships • Joy to the World • O Christmas Tree • O Holy Night • Silent Night • What Child Is This? • and more.

00699493 Guitar Solo.............................. $10.99

FINGERPICKING CHRISTMAS

INCLUDES TAB

Features 20 classic carols for the intermediate-level guitarist. Includes: Away in a Manger • Deck the Hall • The First Noel • It Came upon the Midnight Clear • Jingle Bells • O Come, All Ye Faithful • Silent Night • We Wish You a Merry Christmas • What Child Is This? • and more.

00699599 Solo Guitar.............................. $9.99

FINGERPICKING CHRISTMAS CLASSICS

INCLUDES TAB

15 favorite holiday tunes, with each solo combining melody and harmony in one superb fingerpicking arrangement. Includes: Christmas Time Is Here • Feliz Navidad • I Saw Mommy Kissing Santa Claus • Mistletoe and Holly • My Favorite Things • Santa Baby • Somewhere in My Memory • and more.

00701695 Solo Guitar.............................. $7.99

FINGERPICKING YULETIDE

INCLUDES TAB

Carefully written for intermediate-level guitarists, this collection includes an introduction to fingerstyle guitar and 16 holiday favorites: Do You Hear What I Hear • Happy Xmas (War Is Over) • A Holly Jolly Christmas • Jingle-Bell Rock • Rudolph the Red-Nosed Reindeer • and more.

00699654 Fingerstyle Guitar..................... $9.99

THE ULTIMATE CHRISTMAS GUITAR SONGBOOK

100 songs in a variety of notation styles, from easy guitar and classical guitar arrangements to note-for-note guitar tab transcriptions. Includes: All Through the Night • Auld Lang Syne • Away in a Manger • Blue Christmas • The Chipmunk Song • The Gift • I've Got My Love to Keep Me Warm • Jingle Bells • One Bright Star • Santa Baby • Silver Bells • Wonderful Christmastime • and more.

00700185 Multi-Arrangements.................. $19.95

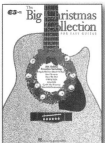

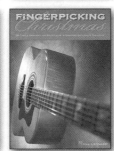
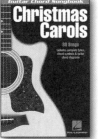

HAL•LEONARD®

www.halleonard.com

Prices, contents and availability subject to change without notice.

AUTHENTIC CHORDS • ORIGINAL KEYS • COMPLETE SONGS

The *Strum It* series lets players strum the chords and sing along with their favorite hits. Each song has been selected because it can be played with regular open chords, barre chords, or other moveable chord types. Guitarists can simply play the rhythm, or play and sing along through the entire song. All songs are shown in their original keys complete with chords, strum patterns, melody and lyrics. Wherever possible, the chord voicings from the recorded versions are notated.

THE BEACH BOYS' GREATEST HITS
00699357.. $12.95

THE BEATLES FAVORITES
00699249..$15.99

VERY BEST OF JOHNNY CASH
00699514..$14.99

CELTIC GUITAR SONGBOOK
00699265..$9.95

CHRISTMAS SONGS FOR GUITAR
00699247..$10.95

CHRISTMAS SONGS WITH 3 CHORDS
00699487..$8.95

VERY BEST OF ERIC CLAPTON
00699560..$12.95

JIM CROCE – CLASSIC HITS
00699269..$10.95

DISNEY FAVORITES
00699171..$12.99

MELISSA ETHERIDGE GREATEST HITS
00699518..$12.99

FAVORITE SONGS WITH 3 CHORDS
00699112..$10.99

FAVORITE SONGS WITH 4 CHORDS
00699270..$8.95

FIRESIDE SING-ALONG
00699273..$10.99

FOLK FAVORITES
00699517..$8.95

THE GUITAR STRUMMERS' ROCK SONGBOOK
00701678..$14.99

BEST OF WOODY GUTHRIE
00699496..$12.95

JOHN HIATT COLLECTION
00699398..$16.99

THE VERY BEST OF BOB MARLEY
00699524..$14.99

A MERRY CHRISTMAS SONGBOOK
00699211..$9.95

MORE FAVORITE SONGS WITH 3 CHORDS
00699532..$9.99

THE VERY BEST OF TOM PETTY
00699336..$12.95

ELVIS! GREATEST HITS
00699276..$10.95

BEST OF GEORGE STRAIT
00699235..$14.99

TAYLOR SWIFT FOR ACOUSTIC GUITAR
00109717..$16.99

BEST OF HANK WILLIAMS JR.
00699224..$15.99

HAL•LEONARD®

Prices, contents & availability subject to change without notice.

Visit Hal Leonard online at
www.halleonard.com

0717

Guitar Chord Songbooks

Each 6" x 9" book includes complete lyrics, chord symbols, and guitar chord diagrams.

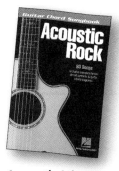
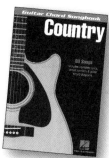
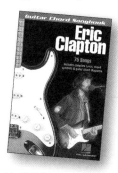
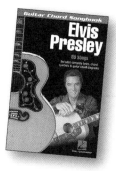

Acoustic Hits
00701787 . . . . $14.99

Acoustic Rock
00699540 . . . . $19.99

Adele
00102761 . . . . $14.99

Alabama
00699914 . . . . $14.95

The Beach Boys
00699566 . . . . $15.99

The Beatles (A-I)
00699558 . . . . $17.99

The Beatles (J-Y)
00699562 . . . . $17.99

Bluegrass
00702585 . . . . $14.99

Johnny Cash
00699648 . . . . $17.99

Steven Curtis Chapman
00700702 . . . . $17.99

Children's Songs
00699539 . . . . $16.99

Christmas Carols
00699536 . . . . $12.99

Christmas Songs – 2nd Edition
00119911 . . . . $14.99

Eric Clapton
00699567 . . . . $16.99

Classic Rock
00699598 . . . . $16.99

Coffeehouse Hits
00703318 . . . . $14.99

Country
00699534 . . . . $14.99

Country Favorites
00700609 . . . . $14.99

Country Hits
00140859 . . . . $14.99

Country Standards
00700608 . . . . $12.95

Cowboy Songs
00699636 . . . . $14.99

Creedence Clearwater Revival
00701786 . . . . $14.99

Crosby, Stills & Nash
00701609 . . . . $12.99

John Denver
02501697 . . . . $14.99

Neil Diamond
00700606 . . . . $14.99

Disney
00701071 . . . . $16.99

The Best of Bob Dylan
14037617 . . . . $17.99

Eagles
00122917 . . . . $16.99

Early Rock
00699916 . . . . $14.99

Folksongs
00699541 . . . . $14.99

Folk Pop Rock
00699651 . . . . $15.99

40 Easy Strumming Songs
00115972 . . . . $14.99

Four Chord Songs
00701611 . . . . $12.99

Glee
00702501 . . . . $14.99

Gospel Hymns
00700463 . . . . $14.99

Grand Ole Opry®
00699885 . . . . $16.95

Grateful Dead
00139461 . . . . $14.99

Green Day
00103074 . . . . $12.99

Guitar Chord Songbook White Pages
00702609 . . . . $29.99

Irish Songs
00701044 . . . . $14.99

Michael Jackson
00137847 . . . . $14.99

Billy Joel
00699632 . . . . $15.99

Elton John
00699732 . . . . $15.99

Ray LaMontagne
00130337 . . . . $12.99

Latin Songs
00700973 . . . . $14.99

Love Songs
00701043 . . . . $14.99

Bob Marley
00701704 . . . . $12.99

Bruno Mars
00125332 . . . . $12.99

Paul McCartney
00385035 . . . . $16.95

Steve Miller
00701146 . . . . $12.99

Modern Worship
00701801 . . . . $16.99

Motown
00699734 . . . . $17.99

Nirvana
00699762 . . . . $16.99

Roy Orbison
00699752 . . . . $14.99

Peter, Paul & Mary
00103013 . . . . $14.99

Tom Petty
00699883 . . . . $15.99

Pink Floyd
00139116 . . . . $14.99

Pop/Rock
00699538 . . . . $14.95

Praise & Worship
00699634 . . . . $14.99

Elvis Presley
00699633 . . . . $14.95

Queen
00702395 . . . . $12.99

Red Hot Chili Peppers
00699710 . . . . $17.99

Rock Ballads
00701034 . . . . $14.99

The Rolling Stones
00137716 . . . . $14.99

Bob Seger
00701147 . . . . $12.99

Carly Simon
00121011 . . . . $14.99

Sting
00699921 . . . . $14.99

Taylor Swift
00701799 . . . . $15.99

Three Chord Acoustic Songs
00123860 . . . . $14.99

Three Chord Songs
00699720 . . . . $14.99

Top 100 Hymns Guitar Songbook
75718017 . . . . $14.99

Two-Chord Songs
00119236 . . . . $14.99

U2
00137744 . . . . $14.99

Hank Williams
00700607 . . . . $14.99

Stevie Wonder
00120862 . . . . $14.99

Neil Young–Decade
00700464 . . . . $14.99

Prices, contents, and availability subject to change without notice.

Visit Hal Leonard online at **www.halleonard.com**

All I Want for Christmas
Is My Two Front Teeth

As Long as There's Christmas

Because It's Christmas
(For All the Children)

Blue Christmas

Caroling, Caroling

The Chipmunk Song

C-H-R-I-S-T-M-A-S

Christmas Is A-Comin'
(May God Bless You)

The Christmas Song
(Chestnuts Roasting on an Open Fire)

Christmas Time Is Here

The Christmas Waltz

Cold December Nights

Do They Know It's Christmas?
(Feed the World)

Do You Hear What I Hear

Do You Want to Build a Snowman?

Emmanuel

Feliz Navidad

The First Chanukah Night

Frosty the Snow Man

The Gift

Give Love on Christmas Day

Glad Tidings (Shalom Chaverim)

Goin' on a Sleighride

Grandma Got Run Over by a Reindeer

Grandma's Killer Fruitcake

The Greatest Gift of All

Greenwillow Christmas

Grown-Up Christmas List

Happy Christmas, Little Friend

Happy Holiday

Happy Xmas (War Is Over)

Have Yourself a Merry Little Christmas

Here Comes Santa Claus
(Right Down Santa Claus Lane)

A Holly Jolly Christmas

Holly Leaves and Christmas Trees

(There's No Place Like)
Home for the Holidays

How Lovely Is Christmas

I Heard the Bells on Christmas Day

I Saw Mommy Kissing Santa Claus

I Still Believe in Santa Claus

I'll Be Home for Christmas

I'll Be Home on Christmas Day

I'm Spending Christmas with You

I've Got My Love to Keep Me Warm

It Must Have Been the Mistletoe
(Our First Christmas)

It Won't Seem Like Christmas
(Without You)

It's Beginning to Look Like Christmas

It's Christmas in New York

It's Christmas Time All Over the World

Jesus Is Born

Jingle Bell Rock

Jingle, Jingle, Jingle

The Last Month of the Year
(What Month Was Jesus Born In?)

Let It Snow! Let It Snow! Let It Snow!

The Little Boy That Santa Claus Forgot

The Little Drummer Boy

Little Saint Nick

A Marshmallow World

Mary, Did You Know?

Merry Christmas, Baby

Merry Christmas, Darling

The Merry Christmas Polka

Merry Christmas Waltz

Merry, Merry Christmas Baby

Miss You Most at Christmas Time

Mister Santa

The Most Wonderful Day of the Year

The Most Wonderful Time of the Year

My Favorite Things

The Night Before Christmas Song

Nuttin' for Christmas

Old Toy Trains

Please Come Home for Christmas

Pretty Paper

Rockin' Around the Christmas Tree

Rudolph The Red-Nosed Reindeer

Santa, Bring My Baby Back (To Me)

Santa Claus Is Comin' to Town

Shake Me I Rattle (Squeeze Me I Cry)

Silver and Gold

Silver Bells

Sleigh Ride

Some Children See Him

Someday at Christmas

Somewhere in My Memory

The Star Carol

Suzy Snowflake

This Christmas

This Is Christmas
(Bright, Bright the Holly Berries)

We Need a Little Christmas

What a Merry Christmas This Could Be

What Are You Doing New Year's Eve?

What Christmas Means to Me

Where Are You Christmas?

White Christmas

The White World of Winter

Why Christmas

Winter Wonderland

Wonderful Christmastime

You Make It Feel Like Christmas

HL00236705

ISBN 978-1-4950-9661-7

51699